William the Conqueror

Makers of History Series

Jacob Abbott

Cedar Lake Classics

Copyright © 2023 by Cedar Lake Classics

This is an annotated edition of a public domain work.

CONTENTS

PREFACE vii
PHOTO INSERT viii

1 Normandy 1

2 Birth of William 12

3 The Accession 24

4 William's Reign in Normandy 36

5 The Marriage 49

6 The Lady Emma 63

7 King Harold 76

8 The Preparations 89

9 Crossing the Channel 103

10 The Battle of Hastings 117

11 Prince Robert's Rebellion 134

12 The Conclusion 148

CONTENTS

ABOUT JACOB ABBOTT   **163**

PREFACE

IN selecting the subjects for the successive volumes of this series, it has been the object of the author to look for the names of those great personages whose histories constitute useful, and not merely entertaining, knowledge. There are certain names which are familiar, as names, to all mankind; and every person who seeks for any degree of mental cultivation, feels desirous of informing himself of the leading outlines of their history, that he may know, in brief, what it was in their characters or their doings which has given them so widely-extended a fame. This knowledge, which it seems incumbent on every one to obtain in respect to such personages as Hannibal, Alexander, Cæsar, Cleopatra, Darius, Xerxes, Alfred, William the Conqueror, Queen Elizabeth, and Mary Queen of Scots, it is the design and object of these volumes to communicate, in a faithful, and, at the same time, if possible, in an attractive manner. Consequently, great historical names alone are selected; and it has been the writer's aim to present the prominent and leading traits in their characters, and all the important events in their lives, in a bold and free manner, and yet in the plain and simple language which is so obviously required in works which aim at permanent and practical usefulness.

William the Conqueror

1

Normandy

A.D. 870-912

The Norman Conquest.—Claim of William to the throne.—The right of the strongest.—Map of Normandy.—The English Channel.—Nature of the French coast.—Nature of the English coast.—Northmen and Danes. —Character of the Northmen.—Their descendants.—The Dukes of Normandy.—The first duke, Rollo.—History of Rollo.—His rendezvous on the Scottish coast.—Expedition of Rollo.—His descent upon Flanders.— Difficulties encountered.—Rollo passes the Straits of Dover.—Charles the Simple.—Defeated by Rollo.—Treaty of peace.—Its conditions.— The three ceremonies.—Rollo's pride.—Kissing the king's foot.—The baptism and marriage.—Rollo's peaceful and prosperous reign.—Description of Normandy.—Scenery.—Hamlets.—Chateaux.—Peasantry.—Public roads.—Rouen.—Its situation.—The port of Rouen.—Its name of Le Havre de Grace.—Intermingling of races.—Superiority of the Norman stock.

ONE of those great events in English history, which occur at distant intervals, and form, respectively, a sort of bound or landmark, to which all other events, preceding or following them for centuries, are referred, is what is called the Norman Conquest. The Norman Conquest was, in fact, the accession of William, duke of Normandy, to the English throne. This accession was not altogether a matter of military force, for William claimed a *right* to the throne, which, if not altogether perfect, was, as he maintained, at any rate superior to that of the prince against whom he contended. The rightfulness of his claim was, however, a matter of little consequence, except so far as the moral influence of it aided him in gaining possession. The right to rule was, in those days, rather more openly and nakedly, though not much more really, than it is now, the right of the strongest.

Normandy, William's native land, is a very rich and beautiful province in the north of France. The following map shows its situation:

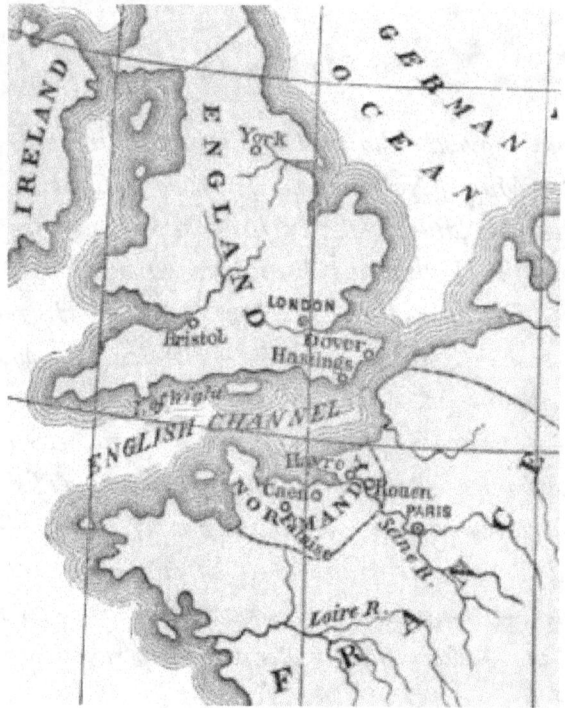

Map of William's Possessions in 1087

It lies, as will be seen upon the map, on the coast of France, adjoining the English Channel. The Channel is here irregular in form, but may be, perhaps, on the average, one hundred miles wide. The line of coast on the southern side of the Channel, which forms, of course, the northern border of Normandy, is a range of cliffs, which are almost perpendicular toward the sea, and which frown forbiddingly upon every ship that sails along the shore. Here and there, it is true, a river opens a passage for itself among these cliffs from the interior, and these river mouths would form harbors into which ships might enter from the offing, were it not that the northwestern winds prevail so generally, and drive such a continual swell of rolling surges in upon the shore, that they choke up all these estuary openings, as well as every natural indentation of the land, with shoals and bars of sand and shingle. The reverse is the case with the northern, or English shore of this famous channel. There the harbors formed by the mouths of the rivers, or by the sinuosities of the shore, are open and accessible, and at the same time sheltered from the winds and the sea. Thus, while the northern or English shore has been, for many centuries, all the time enticing the seaman in and out over the calm, deep, and sheltered waters which there penetrate the land, the southern side has been an almost impassable barrier, consisting of a long line of frowning cliffs, with every opening through it choked with shoals and sand-banks, and guarded by the rolling and tumbling of surges which scarcely ever rest.

It is in a great measure owing to these great physical differences between the two shores, that the people who live upon the one side, though of the same stock and origin with those who live upon the other, have become so vastly superior to them in respect to naval exploits and power. They are really of the same stock and origin, since both England and the northern part of France were overrun and settled by what is called the Scandinavian race, that is, people from Norway, Denmark, and other countries on the Baltic. These people were called the *Northmen* in the histories of those times. Those who landed in England are generally termed *Danes*, though but a small portion of them came really from Denmark. They were all, however, of the same parent stock, and possessed the same qualities of courage, energy, and fearless love of adventure and of danger which distinguish their descendants at the present day. They came down in those early times in great military hordes, and in fleets of piratical ships, through the German Ocean and the various British seas, braving every hardship and every imaginable danger, to find new regions to dwell in, more genial, and fertile, and rich than their own native northern climes. In these days they evince the same energy, and endure equal privations and hardships, in hunting whales in the Pacific Ocean; in overrunning India, and seizing its sources of wealth and power; or in sallying forth, whole fleets of adventurers at a time, to go more than half round the globe, to dig for gold in California. The times and circumstances have changed, but the race and spirit are the same.

Normandy takes its name from the Northmen. It was the province of France which the Northmen made peculiarly their own. They gained access to it from the sea by the River Seine, which, as will be seen from the map, flows, as it were, through the heart of the country. The lower part of this river, and the sea around its mouth, are much choked up with sand and gravel, which the waves have been for ages washing in. Their incessant industry would result in closing up the passage entirely, were it not that the waters of the river must have an outlet; and thus the current, setting outward, wages perpetual war with the surf and surges which are continually breaking in. The expeditions of the Northmen, however, found their way through all these obstructions. They ascended the river with their ships, and finally gained a permanent settlement in the country. They had occupied the country for some centuries at the time when our story begins—the province being governed by a line of princes—almost, if not quite, independent sovereigns—called the *Dukes of Normandy*.

The first Duke of Normandy, and the founder of the line—the chieftain who originally invaded and conquered the country—was a wild and half-savage hero from the north, named *Rollo*. He is often, in history, called Rollo the Dane. Norway was his native land. He was a chieftain by birth there, and, being of a wild and adventurous disposition, he collected a band of followers, and committed with them so many piracies and robberies, that at length the king of the country expelled him.

Rollo seems not to have considered this banishment as any very great calamity, since, far from interrupting his career of piracy and plunder, it only widened the field on which he was to pursue it. He accordingly increased the equipment and the force of his fleet, enlisted more followers, and set sail across the northern part of the German Ocean toward the British shores.

Off the northwestern coast of Scotland there are some groups of mountainous and gloomy islands, which have been, in many different periods of the world, the refuge of fugitives and outlaws. Rollo made these islands his rendezvous now; and he found collected there many other similar spirits, who had fled to these lonely retreats, some on account of political disturbances in which they had become involved, and some on account of their crimes. Rollo's impetuous, ardent, and self-confident character inspired them with new energy and zeal. They gathered around him as their leader. Finding his strength thus increasing, he formed a scheme of concentrating all the force that he could command, so as to organize a grand expedition to proceed to the southward, and endeavor to find some pleasant country which they could seize and settle upon, and make their own. The desperate adventurers around him were ready enough to enter into this scheme. The fleet was refitted, provisioned, and equipped. The expedition was organized, arms and munitions of war provided, and when all was ready they set sail. They had no definite plan in respect to the place of their destination, their intention being to make themselves a home on the first favorable spot that they should find.

They moved southward, cruising at first along the coast of Scotland, and then of England. They made several fruitless attempts to land on the English shores, but were every where repulsed. The time when these events took place was during the reign of Alfred the Great. Through Alfred's wise and efficient measures the whole of his frontier had been put into a perfect state of defense, and Rollo found that there was no hope for him there. He accordingly moved on toward the Straits of Dover; but, before passing them, he made a descent upon the coast of Flanders. Here there was a country named Hainault. It was governed by a potentate called the Count of Hainault. Rollo made war upon him, defeated him in battle, took him prisoner, and then compelled the countess his wife to raise and pay him an immense sum for his ransom. Thus he replenished his treasury by an exploit which was considered in those days very great and glorious. To perpetrate such a deed now, unless it were on a *very* great scale, would be to incur the universal reprobation of mankind; but Rollo, by doing it then, not only enriched his coffers, but acquired a very extended and honorable fame.

For some reason or other, Rollo did not attempt to take permanent possession of Hainault, but, after receiving his ransom money, and replenishing his ammunition and stores, he sailed away with his fleet, and, turning westward, he passed through the Straits of Dover, and cruised along the coast of France. He found that the country on the French side of the channel, though equally rich and beautiful with the opposite shore, was in a very different state of defense. He entered the mouth of the Seine. He was embarrassed at first by the difficulties of the navigation in entering the river; but as there was no efficient enemy to oppose him, he soon triumphed over these difficulties, and, once fairly in the river, he found no difficulty in ascending to Rouen.

In the mean time, the King of France, whose name was Charles, and who is generally designated in history as Charles the Simple, began to collect an army to meet the invader. Rollo, however, had made himself master of Rouen before Charles was able to offer him any effectual opposition. Rouen was already a strong place, but Rollo made it stronger. He enlarged and repaired the fortifications, built store-houses, established a garrison, and, in a word, made all the arrangements requisite for securing an impregnable position for himself and his army.

A long and obstinate war followed between Rollo and Charles, Rollo being almost uniformly victorious in the combats that took place. Rollo became more and more proud and imperious in proportion to his success. He drove the French king from port to port, and from field to field, until he made himself master of a large part of the north of France, over which he gradually established a regular government of his own. Charles struggled in vain to resist these encroachments. Rollo continually defeated him; and finally he shut him up and besieged him in Paris itself. At length Charles was compelled to enter into negotiations for peace. Rollo demanded that the large and rich tract on both sides of the Seine, next the sea—the same, in fact, that now constitutes Normandy—should be ceded to him and his followers for their permanent possession. Charles was extremely unwilling thus to alienate a part of his kingdom. He would not consent to cede it absolutely and entirely, so as to make it an independent realm. It should be a *dukedom*, and not a separate *kingdom*, so that it might continue still a part of his own royal domains—Rollo to reign over it as a duke, and to acknowledge a general allegiance to the French king. Rollo agreed to this. The war had been now protracted so long that he began himself to desire repose. It was more than thirty years since the time of his landing.

Charles had a daughter named Giselle, and it was a part of the treaty of peace that she should become Rollo's wife. He also agreed to become a Christian. Thus there were, in the execution of the treaty, three ceremonies to be performed. First, Rollo was to *do homage*, as it was called, for his duchy; for it was the custom in those days for subordinate princes, who held their possessions of some higher and more strictly sovereign power, to perform certain ceremonies in the presence of their superior lord, which was called doing homage. These ceremonies were of various kinds in different countries, though they were all intended to express the submission of the dependent prince to the superior authority and power of the higher potentate of whom he held his lands. This act of homage was therefore to be performed, and next to the homage was to come the baptism, and after the baptism, the marriage.

When, however, the time came for the performance of the first of these ceremonies, and all the great chieftains and potentates of the respective armies were assembled to witness it, Rollo, it was found, would not submit to what the customs of the French monarchy required. He ought to kneel before the king, and put his hands, clasped together, between the king's hands, in token of submission, and then to kiss his foot, which was covered with an elegantly fashioned slipper on such occasions. Rollo would do all except the last; but that, no remonstrances, urgencies, or persuasions would induce him to consent to.

And yet it was not a very unusual sign or token of political subordination to sovereign power in those days. The pope had exacted it even of an emperor a hundred years before; and it is continued by that dignitary to the present day, on certain state occasions; though in the case of the pope, there is embroidered on the slipper which the kneeling suppliant kisses, a *cross*, so that he who humbles himself to this ceremony may consider, if he pleases, that it is that sacred symbol of the divine Redeemer's sufferings and death that he so reverently kisses, and not the human foot by which it is covered.

Rollo could not be made to consent, himself, to kiss King Charles's foot; and, finally, the difficulty was compromised by his agreeing to do it by proxy. He ordered one of his courtiers to perform that part of the ceremony. The courtier obeyed, but when he came to lift the foot, he did it so rudely and lifted it so high as to turn the monarch over off his seat. This made a laugh, but Rollo was too powerful for Charles to think of resenting it.

A few days after this Rollo was baptized in the cathedral church at Rouen, with great pomp and parade; and then, on the following week, he was married to Giselle. The din of war in which he had lived for more than thirty years was now changed into festivities and rejoicings. He took full and peaceable possession of his dukedom, and governed it for the remainder of his days with great wisdom, and lived in great prosperity. He made it, in fact, one of the richest and most prosperous realms in Europe, and laid the foundations of still higher degrees of greatness and power, which were gradually developed after his death. And this was the origin of Normandy.

It appears thus that this part of France was seized by Rollo and his Northmen partly because it was nearest at hand to them, being accessible from the English Channel through the River Seine, and partly on account of its exceeding richness and fertility. It has been famous in every age as the garden of France, and travelers at the present day gaze upon its picturesque and beautiful scenery with the highest admiration and pleasure. And yet the scenes which are there presented to the view are wholly unlike those which constitute picturesque and beautiful rural scenery in England and America. In Normandy, the land is not inclosed. No hedges, fences, or walls break the continuity of the surface, but vast tracts spread in every direction, divided into plots and squares, of various sizes and forms, by the varieties of cultivation, like a vast carpet of an irregular tesselated pattern, and varied in the color by a thousand hues of brown and green. Here and there vast forests extend, where countless thousands of trees, though ancient and venerable in form, stand in rows, mathematically arranged, as they were planted centuries ago. These are royal demesnes, and hunting grounds, and parks connected with the country palaces of the kings or the chateaux of the ancient nobility. The cultivators of the soil live, not, as in America, in little farmhouses built along the road-sides and dotting the slopes of the hills, but in compact villages, consisting of ancient dwellings of brick or stone, densely packed together along a single street, from which the laborers issue, in picturesque dresses, men and women together, every morning, to go miles, perhaps, to the scene of their daily toil. Except these villages, and the occasional appearance of an ancient chateau, no habitations are seen. The country seems a vast solitude, teeming everywhere, however, with fertility and beauty. The roads which traverse these scenes are magnificent avenues, broad, straight, continuing for many miles an undeviating course over the undulations of the land, with nothing to separate them from the expanse of cultivation and fruitfulness on either hand but rows of ancient and venerable trees. Between these rows of trees the traveler sees an interminable vista extending both before him and behind him. In England, the public road winds beautifully between walls overhung with shrubbery, or hedge-rows, with stiles or gateways here and there, revealing hamlets or cottages, which appear and disappear in a rapid and endlessly varied succession, as the road meanders, like a rivulet, between its beautiful banks. In a word, the public highway in England is beautiful; in France it is grand.

The greatest city in Normandy in modern times is Rouen, which is situated, as will be seen by referring to the map at the commencement of this chapter, on the Seine, half way between Paris and the sea. At the mouth of the Seine, or, rather, on the northern shore of the estuary which forms the mouth of the river, is a small inlet, which has been found to afford, on the whole, the best facilities for a harbor that can be found on the whole line of the coast. Even this little port, however, is so filled up with sand, that when the water recedes at low tide it leaves the shipping all aground. The inlet would, in fact, probably become filled up entirely were it not for artificial means taken to prevent it. There are locks and gateways built in such a manner as to retain a large body of water until the tide is down, and then these gates are opened, and the water is allowed to rush out all together, carrying with it the mud and sand which had begun to accumulate. This haven, being, on the whole, the best and most commodious on the coast, was called *the* harbor, or, as the French expressed it in their language, *le havre*, the word *havre* meaning harbor. In fact, the name was in full *le havre de grace*, as if the Normans considered it a matter of special good luck to have even such a chance of a harbor as this at the mouth of their river. The English world have, however, dropped all except the principal word from this long phrase of designation, and call the port simply Havre.

* * *

From Rollo the line of Dukes of Normandy continued in uninterrupted succession down to the time of William, a period of about a hundred and fifty years. The country increased all the time in wealth, in population, and in prosperity. The original inhabitants were not, however, expelled; they remained as peasants, herdsmen, and agriculturists, while the Norman chieftains settled over them, holding severally large estates of land which William granted them. The races gradually became intermingled, though they continued for many centuries to evince the superior spirit and energy which was infused into the population by the Norman stock. In fact, it is thought by many observers that that superiority continues to the present day.

2

Birth of William

A.D. 912-1033

Castle at Falaise.—Present ruins of the castle.—Scenery of the town and castle.—Wall and buildings.—Watch- towers.—Sentinels.—Enchanting prospect.—Chronological history of the Norman line.—Rollo.—William I., second duke.—Richard I., third duke.—Richard II., fourth duke.—Richard III., fifth duke.—Intrigues of Robert.—He becomes the sixth duke.—Robert and Henry.—William's mother.—Robert's first meeting with Arlotte.—He is captivated.—Robert sends for Arlotte.—Scruples of her father.—Arlotte sent to the castle.—Robert's affection for her.—Birth of William.—The nurse's prediction.—William's childhood.—He is a universal favorite.—Robert determines to visit the Holy Land.—Dangers of the journey.—He makes William his heir.—Surprise of the assembly.—The nobles do homage to William.—William is taken to Paris.—He is presented to the French king.

ALTHOUGH Rouen is now very far before all the other cities of Normandy in point of magnitude and importance, and though Rollo, in his conquest of the country, made it his principal head-quarters and his main stronghold, it did not continue exclusively the residence of the dukes of Normandy in after years. The father of William the Conqueror was Robert, who became subsequently the duke, the sixth in the line. He resided, at the time when William was born, in a great castle at Falaise. Falaise, as will be seen upon the map, is west of Rouen, and it stands, like Rouen, at some distance from the sea. The castle was built upon a hill, at a little distance from the town. It has long since ceased to be habitable, but the ruins still remain, giving a picturesque but mournful beauty to the eminence which they crown. They are often visited by travelers, who go to see the place where the great hero and conqueror was born.

The hill on which the old castle stands terminates, on one side, at the foot of the castle walls, in a precipice of rocks, and on two other sides, also, the ascent is too steep to be practicable for an enemy. On the fourth side there is a more gradual declivity, up which the fortress could be approached by means of a winding roadway. At the foot of this roadway was the town. The access to the castle from the town was defended by a ditch and draw-bridge, with strong towers on each side of the gateway to defend the approach. There was a beautiful stream of water which meandered along through the valley, near the town, and, after passing it, it disappeared, winding around the foot of the precipice which the castle crowned. The castle inclosures were shut in with walls of stone of enormous thickness; so thick, in fact, they were, that some of the apartments were built in the body of the wall. There were various buildings within the inclosure. There was, in particular, one large, square tower, several stories in height, built of white stone. This tower, it is said, still stands in good preservation. There was a chapel, also, and various other buildings and apartments within the walls, for the use of the ducal family and their numerous retinue of servants and attendants, for the storage of munitions of war, and for the garrison. There were watch-towers on the corners of the walls, and on various lofty projecting pinnacles, where solitary sentinels watched, the livelong day and night, for any approaching danger. These sentinels looked down on a broad expanse of richly-cultivated country, fields beautified with groves of trees, and with the various colors presented by the changing vegetation, while meandering streams gleamed with their silvery radiance among them, and hamlets of laborers and peasantry were scattered here and there, giving life and animation to the scene.

We have said that William's father was Robert, the sixth Duke of Normandy, so that William himself, being his immediate successor, was the seventh in the line. And as it is the design of these narratives not merely to amuse the reader with what is entertaining as a tale, but to impart substantial historical knowledge, we must prepare the way for the account of William's birth, by presenting a brief chronological view of the whole ducal line, extending from Rollo to William. We recommend to the reader to examine with special attention this brief account of William's ancestry, for the true causes which led to William's invasion of England can not be fully appreciated without thoroughly understanding certain important transactions in which some members of the family of his ancestors were concerned before he was born. This is particularly the case with the Lady Emma, who, as will be seen by the following summary, was the sister of the third duke in the line. The extraordinary and eventful history of her life is so intimately connected with the subsequent exploits of William, that it is necessary to relate it in full, and it becomes, accordingly, the subject of one of the subsequent chapters of this volume.

Chronological History of the Norman Line.

ROLLO, first Duke of Normandy. From A.D. 912 to A.D. 917. It was about 870 that Rollo was banished from Norway, and a few years after that, at most, that he landed in France. It was not, however, until 912 that he concluded his treaty of peace with Charles, so as to be fully invested with the title of Duke of Normandy. He was advanced in age at this time, and, after spending five years in settling the affairs of his realm, he resigned his dukedom into the hands of his son, that he might spend the remainder of his days in rest and peace. He died in 922, five years after his resignation.

WILLIAM I., second Duke of Normandy. From 917 to 942. William was Rollo's son. He began to reign, of course, five years before his father's death. He had a quiet and prosperous reign of about twenty-five years, but he was assassinated at last by a political enemy, in 942.

RICHARD I., third Duke of Normandy. From 942 to 996. He was only ten years old when his father was assassinated. He became involved in long and arduous wars with the King of France, which compelled him to call in the aid of more Northmen from the Baltic. His new allies, in the end, gave him as much trouble as the old enemy, with whom they came to help William contend; and he found it very hard to get them away. He wanted, at length, to make peace with the French king, and to have them leave his dominions; but they said, "That was not what they came for." Richard had a beautiful daughter, named Emma, who afterward became a very important political personage, as will be seen more fully in a subsequent chapter. Richard died in 996, after reigning fifty-four years.

RICHARD II., fourth Duke of Normandy. From 996 to 1026. Richard II. was the son of Richard I., and as his father had been engaged during his reign in contentions with his sovereign lord, the King of France, he, in his turn, was harassed by long-continued struggles with his vassals, the barons and nobles of his own realm. He, too, sent for Northmen to come and assist him. During his reign there was a great contest in England between the Saxons and the Danes, and Ethelred, who was the Saxon claimant to the throne, came to Normandy, and soon afterward married the Lady Emma, Richard's sister. The particulars of this event, from which the most momentous consequences were afterward seen to flow, will be given in full in a future chapter. Richard died in 1026. He left two sons, Richard and Robert. William the Conqueror was the son of the youngest, and was born two years before this Richard II. died.

RICHARD III., fifth Duke of Normandy. From 1026 to 1028. He was the oldest brother, and, of course, succeeded to the dukedom. His brother Robert was then only a baron—his son William, afterward the Conqueror, being then about two years old. Robert was very ambitious and aspiring, and eager to get possession of the dukedom himself. He adopted every possible means to circumvent and supplant his brother, and, as is supposed, shortened his days by the anxiety and vexation which he caused him; for Richard died suddenly and mysteriously only two years after his accession. It was supposed by some, in fact, that he was poisoned, though there was never any satisfactory proof of this.

ROBERT, sixth Duke of Normandy. From 1028 to 1035. Robert, of course, succeeded his brother, and then, with the characteristic inconsistency of selfishness and ambition, he employed all the power of his realm in helping the King of France to subdue his younger brother, who was evincing the same spirit of seditiousness and insubmission that he had himself displayed. His assistance was of great importance to King Henry; it, in fact, decided the contest in his favor; and thus one younger brother was put down in the commencement of his career of turbulence and rebellion, by another who had successfully accomplished a precisely similar course of crime. King Henry was very grateful for the service thus rendered, and was ready to do all in his power, at all times, to co-operate with Robert in the plans which the latter might form. Robert died in 1035, when William was about eleven years old.

And here we close this brief summary of the history of the ducal line, as we have already passed the period of William's birth; and we return, accordingly, to give in detail some of the particulars of that event.

William and Arlotte

* * *

Although the dukes of Normandy were very powerful potentates, reigning, as they did, almost in the character of independent sovereigns, over one of the richest and most populous territories of the globe, and though William the Conqueror was the son of one of them, his birth was nevertheless very ignoble. His mother was not the wife of Robert his father, but a poor peasant girl, the daughter of an humble tanner of Falaise; and, indeed, William's father, Robert, was not himself the duke at this time, but a simple baron, as his father was still living. It was not even certain that he ever would be the duke, as his older brother, who, of course, would come before him, was also then alive. Still, as the son and prospective heir of the reigning duke, his rank was very high.

The circumstances of Robert's first acquaintance with the tanner's daughter were these. He was one day returning home to the castle from some expedition on which he had been sent by his father, when he saw a group of peasant girls standing on the margin of the brook, washing clothes. They were barefooted, and their dress was in other respects disarranged. There was one named Arlotte, [Her name is spelled variously,

Arlette, Arlotte, Harlotte, and in other ways.] the daughter of a tanner of the town, whose countenance and figure seem to have captivated the young baron. He gazed at her with admiration and pleasure as he rode along. Her complexion was fair, her eyes full and blue, and the expression of her countenance was frank, and open, and happy. She was talking joyously and merrily with her companions as Robert passed, little dreaming of the conspicuous place on the page of English history which she was to occupy, in all future time, in connection with the gay horseman who was riding by.

The etiquette of royal and ducal palaces and castles in those days, as now, forbade that a noble of such lofty rank should marry a peasant girl. Robert could not, therefore, have Arlotte for his wife; but there was nothing to prevent his proposing her coming to the castle and living with him—that is, nothing but the law of God, and this was an authority to which dukes and barons in the Middle Ages were accustomed to pay very little regard. There was not even a public sentiment to forbid this, for a nobility like that of England and France in the Middle Ages stands so far above all the mass of society as to be scarcely amenable at all to the ordinary restrictions and obligations of social life. And even to the present day, in those countries where dukes exist, public sentiment seems to tolerate pretty generally whatever dukes see fit to do.

Accordingly, as soon as Robert had arrived at the castle, he sent a messenger from his retinue of attendants down to the village, to the father of Arlotte, proposing that she should come to the castle. The father seems to have had some hesitation in respect to his duty. It is said that he had a brother who was a monk, or rather hermit, who lived a life of reading, meditation and prayer, in a solitary place not far from Falaise. Arlotte's father sent immediately to this religious recluse for his spiritual counsel. The monk replied that it was right to comply with the wishes of so great a man, whatever they might be. The tanner, thus relieved of all conscientious scruples on the subject by this high religious authority, and rejoicing in the opening tide of prosperity and distinction which he foresaw for his family through the baron's love, robed and decorated his daughter, like a lamb for the sacrifice, and sent her to the castle.

Arlotte had one of the rooms assigned her, which was built in the thickness of the wall. It communicated by a door with the other apartments and enclosures within the area, and there were narrow windows in the masonry without, through which she could look out over the broad expanse of beautiful fields and meadows which were smiling below. Robert seems to have loved her with sincere and strong affection, and to have done all in his power to make her happy. Her room, however, could not have been very sumptuously furnished, although she was the favorite in a ducal castle—at least so far as we can judge from the few glimpses we get of the interior through the ancient chroniclers' stories. One story is, that when William was born, his first exploit was to grasp a handful of straw, and to hold it so tenaciously in his little fist that the nurse could scarcely take it away. The nurse was greatly delighted with this infantile prowess; she considered it an omen, and predicted that the babe would someday signalize himself by seizing and holding great possessions. The prediction would have been forgotten if William had not become the conqueror of England at a future day. As it was, it was remembered and recorded; and it suggests to our imagination a very different picture of the conveniences and comforts of Arlotte's chamber from those presented to the eye in ducal palaces now, where carpets of velvet silence the tread on marble floors, and favorites repose under silken canopies on beds of down.

The babe was named William, and he was a great favorite with his father. He was brought up at Falaise. Two years after his birth, Robert's father died, and his oldest brother, Richard III., succeeded to the ducal throne. In two years more, which years were spent in contention between the brothers, Richard also died, and then Robert himself came into possession of the castle in his own name, reigning there over all the cities and domains of Normandy.

William was, of course, now about four years old. He was a bright and beautiful boy, and he grew more and more engaging every year.

His father, instead of neglecting and disowning him, as it might have been supposed he would do, took a great deal of pride and pleasure in witnessing the gradual development of his powers and his increasing attractiveness, and he openly acknowledged him as his son.

In fact, William was a universal favorite about the castle. When he was five and six years old he was very fond of playing the soldier. He would marshal the other boys of the castle, his playmates, into a little troop, and train them around the castle enclosures, just as ardent and aspiring boys do with their comrades now. He possessed a certain vivacity and spirit too, which gave him, even then, a great ascendency over his playfellows. He invented their plays; he led them in their mischief; he settled their disputes. In a word, he possessed a temperament and character which enabled him very easily and strongly to hold the position which his rank as son of the lord of the castle so naturally assigned him.

A few years thus passed away, when, at length, Robert conceived the design of making a pilgrimage to the Holy Land. This was a plan, not of humble-minded piety, but of ambition for fame. To make a pilgrimage to the Holy Land was a romantic achievement that covered whoever accomplished it with a sort of sombre glory, which, in the case of a prince or potentate, mingled with, and hallowed and exalted, his military renown. Robert determined on making the pilgrimage. It was a distant and dangerous journey. In fact, the difficulties and dangers of the way were perhaps what chiefly imparted to the enterprise its romance, and gave it its charms. It was customary for kings and rulers, before setting out, to arrange all the affairs of their kingdoms, to provide a regency to govern during their absence, and to determine upon their successors, so as to provide for the very probable contingency of their not living to return.

As soon, therefore, as Robert announced his plan of a pilgrimage, men's minds were immediately turned to the question of the succession. Robert had never been married, and he had consequently no son who was entitled to succeed him. He had two brothers, and also a cousin, and some other relatives, who had claims to the succession. These all began to maneuver among the chieftains and nobles, each endeavoring to prepare the way for having his own claims advanced, while Robert himself was secretly determining that the little William should be his heir. He said nothing about this, however, but he took care to magnify the importance of his little son in every way, and to bring him as much as possible into public notice. William, on his part, possessed so much personal beauty, and so many juvenile accomplishments, that he became a great favorite with all the nobles, and chieftains, and knights who saw him, sometimes at his father's castle, and sometimes away from home, in their own fortresses or towns, where his father took him, from time to time, in his train.

At length, when affairs were ripe for their consummation, Duke Robert called together a grand council of all the subordinate dukes, and earls, and barons of his realm, to make known to them the plan of his pilgrimage. They came together from all parts of Normandy, each in a splendid cavalcade, and attended by an armed retinue of retainers. When the assembly had been convened, and the preliminary forms and ceremonies had been disposed of, Robert announced his grand design.

As soon as he had concluded, one of the nobles, whose name and title was Guy, count of Burgundy, rose and addressed the duke in reply. He was sorry, he said, to hear that the duke, his cousin, entertained such a plan. He feared for the safety of the realm when the chief ruler should be gone. All the estates of the realm, he said, the barons, the knights, the chieftains and soldiers of every degree, would be all without a head.

"Not so," said Robert: "I will leave you a master in my place." Then, pointing to the beautiful boy by his side, he added, "I have a little fellow here, who, though he is little now, I acknowledge, will grow bigger by and by, with God's grace, and I have great hopes that he will become a brave and gallant man. I present him to you, and from this time forth I give him *seizin [Seizin, an ancient feudal term denoting the inducting of a party to a legal possession of his right.]* of the Duchy of Normandy as my known and acknowledged heir. And I appoint Alan, duke of

Brittany, governor of Normandy in my name until I shall return, and in case I shall not return, in the name of William my son, until he shall become of manly age."

The assembly was taken wholly by surprise at this announcement. Alan, duke of Brittany, who was one of the chief claimants to the succession, was pleased with the honor conferred upon him in making him at once the governor of the realm, and was inclined to prefer the present certainty of governing at once in the name of others, to the remote contingency of reigning in his own. The other claimants to the inheritance were confounded by the suddenness of the emergency, and knew not what to say or do. The rest of the assembly were pleased with the romance of having the beautiful boy for their feudal sovereign. The duke saw at once that every thing was favorable to the accomplishment of his design. He took the lad in his arms, kissed him, and held him out in view of the assembly. William gazed around upon the panoplied warriors before him with a bright and beaming eye. They knelt down as by a common accord to do him homage, and then took the oath of perpetual allegiance and fidelity to his cause.

Robert thought, however, that it would not be quite prudent to leave his son himself in the custody of these his rivals, so he took him with him to Paris when he set out upon his pilgrimage, with view of establishing him there, in the court of Henry, the French king, while he should himself be gone. Young William was presented to the French king, on a day set apart for the ceremony, with great pomp and parade. The king held a special court to receive him. He seated himself on his throne in a grand apartment of his palace, and was surrounded by his nobles and officers of state, all magnificently dressed for the occasion. At the proper time, Duke Robert came in, dressed in his pilgrim's garb, and leading young William by the hand. His attendant pilgrim knights accompanied him. Robert led the boy to the feet of their common sovereign, and, kneeling there, ordered William to kneel too, to do homage to the king. King Henry received him very graciously. He embraced him, and promised to receive him into his court, and to take the best possible care of him while his father was away. The courtiers were very much struck with the beauty and noble bearing of the boy. His countenance beamed with an animated, but yet very serious expression, as he was somewhat awed by the splendor of the scene around him. He was himself then nine years old.

3

The Accession

A.D. 1035-1040

Robert departs on his pilgrimage.—He visits Rome and Constantinople. —Robert's illness.—Litter bearers.—Death of Robert.—Claimants to the crown.—Theroulde.—William's military education.—The Earl of Arques.—William proclaimed duke.—The pilgrim knights.—They embrace William's cause.—Debates in the council on the propriety of William's return.—William's return to Normandy.—Its effects.—William's accomplishments.—Impression upon the army.—Claimants in the field.— Iron rule of the nobles.—Almost a quarrel.—Interview between William and Henry.—Henry's demand.—William's indignation.—Henry destroys one of William's castles.—Difficulties which followed.—War with Henry.—William rescues Falaise.—William received with acclamations.—Punishment of the governor.—The Earl of Arques.—Advance of Henry.—A dangerous defile.—Henry's order of march.—William's ambuscade.—Its success.—Pretended flight of the Normans.—Disarray of the French.—Rout of the French.—William's embassage to Henry.— The castle at Arques taken.—William crowned at Falaise.

AFTER spending a little time at Paris, Robert took leave of the king, and of William his son, and went forth, with a train of attendant knights, on his pilgrimage. He had a great variety of adventures, which can not be related here, as it is the history of the son, and not of the father, which is the subject of this narrative. Though he traveled strictly as a pilgrim, it was still with great pomp and parade. After visiting Rome, and accomplishing various services and duties connected with his pilgrimage there, he laid aside his pilgrim's garb, and, assuming his proper rank as a great Norman chieftain, he went to Constantinople, where he made a great display of his wealth and magnificence. At the time of the grand procession, for example, by which he entered the city of Constantinople, he rode a mule, which, besides being gorgeously caparisoned, had shoes of gold instead of iron; and these shoes were purposely attached so slightly to the hoofs, that they were shaken off as the animal walked along, to be picked up by the populace. This was to impress them with grand ideas of the rider's wealth and splendor. After leaving Constantinople, Robert resumed his pilgrim's garb, and went on toward the Holy Land.

The journey, however, did not pass without the usual vicissitudes of so long an absence and so distant a pilgrimage. At one time Robert was sick, and, after lingering for some time in a fever, he so far recovered his strength as to be borne on a litter by the strength of other men, though he could not advance himself, either on horseback or on foot; and as for traveling carriages, there had been no such invention in those days. They made arrangements, therefore, for carrying the duke on a litter. There were sixteen Moorish slaves employed to serve as his bearers. This company was divided into sets, four in each, the several sets taking the burden in rotation. Robert and his attendant knights looked down with great contempt on these black pagan slaves. One day the cavalcade was met by a Norman who was returning home to Normandy after having accomplished his pilgrimage. He asked Duke Robert if he had any message to send to his friends at home. "Yes," said he; "tell them you saw me here, on my way to Paradise, carried by sixteen *demons*."

Robert reached Jerusalem, and set out on his return; and soon after rumors came back to Paris that he had died on his way home. The accounts of the manner of his death were contradictory and uncertain;

but the fact was soon made sure, and the news produced every where a great sensation. It soon appeared that the brothers and cousins of Robert, who had claimed the right to succeed him in preference to his son William, had only suspended their claims—they had not abandoned them. They began to gather their forces, each in his own separate domain, and to prepare to take the field, if necessary, in vindication of what they considered their rights to the inheritance. In a word, their oaths of fealty to William were all forgotten, and each claimant was intent only on getting possession himself of the ducal crown.

In the mean time, William himself was at Paris, and only eleven years of age. He had been receiving a careful education there, and was a very prepossessing and accomplished young prince. Still, he was yet but a mere boy. He had been under the care of a military tutor, whose name was Theroulde. Theroulde was a veteran soldier, who had long been in the employ of the King of France. He took great interest in his young pupil's progress. He taught him to ride and to practice all the evolutions of horsemanship which were required by the tactics of those days. He trained him, too, in the use of arms, the bow and arrow, the javelin, the sword, the spear, and accustomed him to wear, and to exercise in, the armor of steel with which warriors were used, in those days, to load themselves in going into battle. Young princes like William had suits of this armor made for them, of small size, which they were accustomed to wear in private in their military exercises and trainings, and to appear in, publicly, on great occasions of state. These dresses of iron were of course very heavy and uncomfortable, but the young princes and dukes were, nevertheless, very proud and happy to wear them.

While William was thus engaged in pursuing his military education in Paris, several competitors for his dukedom immediately appeared in Normandy and took the field. The strongest and most prominent among them was the Earl of Arques. His name was William too, but, to distinguish him from the young duke, we shall call him Arques. He was a brother of Robert, and maintained that, as Robert left no lawful heir, he was indisputably entitled to succeed him. Arques assembled his forces and prepared to take possession of the country.

It will be recollected that Robert, when he left Normandy in setting out on his pilgrimage, had appointed a nobleman named Alan to act as regent, or governor of the country, until he should return; or, in case he should never return, until William should become of age. Alan had a council of officers, called the council of regency, with whose aid he managed the administration of the government. This council, with Alan at their head, proclaimed young William duke, and immediately began to act in his name. When they found that the Earl of Arques was preparing to seize the government, they began to assemble their forces also, and thus both sides prepared for war.

Before they actually commenced hostilities, however, the pilgrim knights who had accompanied Robert on his pilgrimage, and who had been journeying home slowly by themselves ever since their leader's death, arrived in Normandy. These were chieftains and nobles of high rank and influence, and each of the contending parties were eager to have them join their side. Besides the actual addition of force which these men could bring to the cause they should espouse, the moral support they would give to it was a very important consideration. Their having been on this long and dangerous pilgrimage invested them with a sort of romantic and religious interest in the minds of all the people, who looked up to them, in consequence of it, with a sort of veneration and awe; and then, as they had been selected by Robert to accompany him on his pilgrimage, and had gone on the long and dangerous journey with him, continuing to attend upon him until he died, they were naturally regarded as his most faithful and confidential friends. For these and similar reasons, it was obvious that the cause which they should espouse in the approaching contest would gain a large accession of moral power by their adhesion.

As soon as they arrived in Normandy, rejecting all proposals from other quarters, they joined young William's cause with the utmost promptitude and decision. Alan received them at once into his councils.

An assembly was convened, and the question was discussed whether William should be sent for to come to Normandy. Some argued that he was yet a mere boy, incapable of rendering them any real service in the impending contest, while he would be exposed, more perhaps than they themselves, to be taken captive or slain. They thought it best, therefore, that he should remain, for the present, in Paris, under the protection of the French king.

Others, on the other hand, contended that the influence of William's presence, boy as he was, would animate and inspire all his followers, and awaken everywhere, throughout the country, a warm interest in his cause; that his very tenderness and helplessness would appeal strongly to every generous heart, and that his youthful accomplishments and personal charms would enlist thousands in his favor, who would forget, and perhaps abandon him, if he kept away. Besides, it was by no means certain that he was so safe as some might suppose in King Henry's custody and power. King Henry might himself lay claims to the vacant duchy, with a view of bestowing it upon some favorite of his own, in which case he might confine young William in one of his castles, in an honorable, but still rigid and hopeless captivity, or treacherously destroy his life by the secret administration of poison.

These latter counsels prevailed. Alan and the nobles who were with him sent an embassage to the court of King Henry to bring William home. Henry made objections and difficulties. This alarmed the nobles. They feared that it would prove true that Henry himself had designs on Normandy. They sent a new embassage, with demands more urgent than before. Finally, after some time spent in negotiations and delays, King Henry concluded to yield, and William set out on his return. He was now about twelve or thirteen years old. His military tutor, Theroulde, accompanied him, and he was attended likewise by the ambassadors whom Alan had sent for him, and by a strong escort for his protection by the way. He arrived in safety at Alan's headquarters.

William's presence in Normandy had the effect which had been anticipated from it. It awakened everywhere a great deal of enthusiasm in his favor. The soldiers were pleased to see how handsome their young commander was in form, and how finely he could ride. He was, in fact, a very superior equestrian for one so young. He was more fond, even, than other boys of horses; and as, of course, the most graceful and the fleetest horses which could be found were provided for him, and as Theroulde had given him the best and most complete instruction, he made a fine display as he rode swiftly through the camp, followed by veteran nobles, splendidly dressed and mounted, and happy to be in his train, while his own countenance beamed with a radiance in which native intelligence and beauty were heightened by the animation and excitement of pride and pleasure. In respect to the command of the army, of course the real power remained in Alan's hands, but everything was done in William's name; and in respect to all external marks and symbols of sovereignty, the beautiful boy seemed to possess the supreme command; and as the sentiment of loyalty is always the strongest when the object which calls for the exercise of it is most helpless or frail, Alan found his power very much increased when he had this beautiful boy to exhibit as the true and rightful heir, in whose name and for whose benefit all his power was held.

Still, however, the country was very far from becoming settled. The Earl of Arques kept the field, and other claimants, too, strengthened themselves in their various castles and towns, as if preparing to resist. In those days, every separate district of the country was almost a separate realm, governed by its own baron, who lived, with his retainers, within his own castle walls, and ruled the land around him with a rod of iron. These barons were engaged in perpetual quarrels among themselves, each plundering the dominions of the rest, or making hostile incursions into the territories of a neighbor to revenge some real or imaginary wrong. This turbulence and disorder prevailed everywhere throughout Normandy at the time of William's return. In the general confusion, William's government scarcely knew who were his friends or his enemies. At one time, when a deputation was sent to some of the barons in William's name, summoning them to come with their forces and join his standard, as they were in duty bound to do, they felt independent enough to send back word to him that they had "too much to do in settling their own quarrels to be able to pay any attention to his."

In the course of a year or two, moreover, and while his own realm continued in this unsettled and distracted state, William became involved in what was almost a quarrel with King Henry himself. When he was fifteen years old, which was two or three years after his return from Paris to Normandy, Henry sent directions to William to come to a certain town, called Evreux, situated about half way between Falaise and Paris, and just within the confines of Normandy, to do homage to him there for his duchy. There was some doubt among William's counselors whether it would be most prudent to obey or disobey this command. They finally concluded that it was best to obey. Grand preparations were accordingly made for the expedition; and, when all was ready, the young duke was conducted in great state, and with much pomp and parade, to meet his sovereign.

The interview between William and his sovereign, and the ceremonies connected with it, lasted some days. In the course of this time, William remained at Evreux, and was, in some sense, of course, in Henry's power. William, having been so long in Henry's court as a mere boy, accustomed all the time to look up to and obey Henry as a father, regarded him somewhat in that light now, and approached him with great deference and respect. Henry received him in a somewhat haughty and imperious manner, as if he considered him still under the same subjection as heretofore.

William had a fortress or castle on the frontiers of his dukedom, toward Henry's dominions. The name of the castle was Tellières, and the governor of it was a faithful old soldier named De Crespin. William's father, Robert, had entrusted De Crespin with the command of the castle, and given him a garrison to defend it. Henry now began to make complaint to William in respect to this castle. The garrison, he said, were continually making incursions into his dominions. William replied that he was very sorry that there was cause for such a complaint. He would inquire into it, and if the fact were really so, he would have the evil immediately corrected. Henry replied that that was not sufficient. "You must deliver up the castle to me," he said, "to be destroyed." William was indignant at such a demand; but he was so accustomed to obey implicitly whatever King Henry might require of him, that he sent the order to have the castle surrendered.

When, however, the order came to De Crespin, the governor of the castle, he refused to obey it. The fortress, he said, had been committed to his charge by Robert, duke of Normandy, and he should not give it up to the possession of any foreign power. When this answer was reported to William and his counselors, it made them still more indignant than before at the domineering tyranny of the command, and more disposed than ever to refuse obedience to it. Still William was in a great measure in the monarch's power. On cool reflection, they perceived that resistance would then be vain. New and more authoritative orders were accordingly issued for the surrender of the castle. De Crespin now obeyed. He gave up the keys and withdrew with his garrison. William was then allowed to leave Evreux and return home, and soon afterward the castle was razed to the ground.

This affair produced, of course, a great deal of animosity and irritation between the governments of France and Normandy; and where such a state of feeling exists between two powers separated only by an imaginary line running through a populous and fertile country, aggressions from one side and from the other are sure to follow. These are soon succeeded by acts of retaliation and revenge, leading, in the end, to an open and general war. It was so now. Henry marched his armies into Normandy, seized towns, destroyed castles, and, where he was resisted by the people, he laid waste the country with fire and sword. He finally laid siege to the very castle of Falaise.

William and his government were for a time nearly overwhelmed with the tide of disaster and calamity. The tide turned, however, at length, and the fortune of war inclined in their favor. William rescued the town and castle of Falaise; it was in a very remarkable manner, too, that this exploit was accomplished. The fortress was closely invested with Henry's forces, and was on the very eve of being surrendered. The story is, that Henry had offered bribes to the governor of the castle to give it up to him, and that the governor had agreed to receive them and to betray his trust. While he was preparing to do so, William arrived at the head of a resolute and determined band of Normans. They came with so sudden an onset upon the army of besiegers as to break up their camp and force them to abandon the siege. The people of the town and the garrison of the castle were extremely rejoiced to be thus rescued, and when they came to learn through whose instrumentality they had been saved, and saw the beautiful horseman whom they remembered as a gay and happy child playing about the precincts of the castle, they were perfectly intoxicated with delight. They filled the air with the wildest acclamations, and welcomed William back to the home of his childhood with manifestations of the most extravagant joy. As to the traitorous governor, he was dealt with very leniently. Perhaps the general feeling of joy awakened emotions of leniency and forgiveness in William's mind—or perhaps the proof against the betrayer was incomplete. They did not, therefore, take his life, which would have been justly forfeited, according to the military ideas of the times, if he had been really guilty. They deprived him of his command, confiscated his property, and let him go free.

After this, William's forces continued for some time to make head successfully against those of the King of France; but then, on the other hand, the danger from his uncle, the Earl of Arques, increased. The earl took advantage of the difficulty and danger in which William was involved in his contests with King Henry, and began to organize his forces again. He fortified himself in his castle at Arques, and was collecting a large force there. Arques was in the northeastern part of Normandy, near the sea, where the ruins of the ancient castle still remain. The earl built an almost impregnable tower for himself on the summit of the rock on which the castle stood, in a situation so inaccessible that he thought he could retreat to it in any emergency, with a few chosen followers, and bid defiance to any assault. In and around this castle the earl had got quite a large army together. William advanced with his forces, and, encamping around them, shut them in. King Henry, who was then in a distant part of Normandy, began to put his army in motion to come to the rescue of Arques.

Things being in this state, William left a strong body of men to continue the investment and siege of Arques, and went off himself, at the head of the remainder of his force, to intercept Henry on his advance. The result was a battle and a victory, gained under circumstances so extraordinary, that William, young as he was, acquired by his exploits a brilliant and universal renown.

It seems that Henry, in his progress to Arques, had to pass through a long and gloomy valley, which was bounded on either side by precipitous and forest-covered hills. Through this dangerous defile the long train of Henry's army was advancing, arranged and marshaled in such an order as seemed to afford the greatest hope of security in case of an attack. First came the vanguard, a strong escort, formed of heavy bodies of soldiery, armed with battle-axes and pikes, and other similar weapons, the most efficient then known. Immediately after this vanguard came a long train of baggage, the tents, the provisions, the stores, and all the munitions of war. The baggage was followed by a great company of servants—the cooks, the carters, the laborers, the camp followers of every description—a throng of non-combatants, useless, of course, in a battle, and a burden on a march, and yet the inseparable and indispensable attendant of an army, whether at rest or in motion. After this throng came the main body of the army, with the king, escorted by his guard of honor, at the head of it. An active and efficient corps of lancers and men-at-arms brought up the rear.

William conceived the design of drawing this cumbrous and unmanageable body into an ambuscade. He selected, accordingly, the narrowest and most dangerous part of the defile for the purpose, and stationed vast numbers of Norman soldiers, armed with javelins and arrows, upon the slopes of the hill on either side, concealing them all carefully among the thickets and rocks. He then marshaled the remainder of his forces in the valley, and sent them up the valley to meet Henry as he was descending. This body of troops, which was to advance openly to meet the king, as if they constituted the whole of William's force, were to fight a pretended battle with the vanguard, and then to retreat, in hopes to draw the whole train after them in a pursuit so eager as to throw them into confusion; and then, when the column, thus disarranged, should reach the place of ambuscade, the Normans were to come down upon them suddenly from their hiding-places, and complete their discomfiture.

The plan was well laid, and wisely and bravely executed; and it was most triumphantly successful in its result. The vanguard of Henry's army were deceived by the pretended flight of the Norman detachment. They supposed, too, that it constituted the whole body of their enemies. They pressed forward, therefore, with great exultation and eagerness to pursue them. News of the attack, and of the apparent repulse with which the French soldiers had met it, passed rapidly along the valley, producing everywhere the wildest excitement, and an eager desire to press forward to the scene of conflict. The whole valley was filled with shouts and outcries; baggage was abandoned, that those who had charge of it might hurry on; men ran to and fro for tidings, or ascended eminences to try to see. Horsemen drove at full speed from front to rear, and from rear on to the front again; orders and counter orders were given, which nobody would understand or attend to in the general confusion and din. In fact, the universal attention seemed absorbed in one general and eager desire to press forward with headlong impetuosity to the scene of victory and pursuit which they supposed was enacting in the van.

The army pressed on in this confused and excited manner until they reached the place of ambuscade. They went on, too, through this narrow passage, as heedlessly as ever; and, when the densest and most powerful portion of the column was crowding through, they were suddenly thunderstruck by the issuing of a thousand weapons from the heights and thickets above them on either hand—a dreadful shower of arrows, javelins, and spears, which struck down hundreds in a moment, and overwhelmed the rest with astonishment and terror. As soon as this first discharge had been effected, the concealed enemy came pouring down the sides of the mountain, springing out from a thousand hiding-places, as if suddenly brought into being by some magic power. The discomfiture of Henry's forces was complete and irremediable. The men fled everywhere in utter dismay, trampling upon and destroying one another, as they crowded back in terrified throngs to find some place of safety up the valley. There, after a day or two, Henry got together the scattered remains of his army, and established something like a camp.

It is a curious illustration of the feudal feelings of those times in respect to the gradation of ranks, or else of the extraordinary modesty and good sense of William's character, that he assumed no airs of superiority over his sovereign, and showed no signs of extravagant elation after this battle. He sent a respectful embassage to Henry, recognizing his own acknowledged subjection to Henry as his sovereign, and imploring his protection! He looked confidently to him, he said, for aid and support against his rebellious subjects.

Though he thus professed, however, to rely on Henry, he really trusted most, it seems, to his own right arm; for, as soon as this battle was fairly over, and while the whole country was excited with the astonishing brilliancy of the exploit performed by so young a man, William mounted his horse, and calling upon those to follow him who wished to do so, he rode at full speed, at the head of a small cavalcade, to the castle at Arques. His sudden appearance here, with the news of the victory, inspirited the besiegers to such a degree that the castle was soon taken. He allowed the rebel earl to escape, and thus, perhaps, all the more effectually put an end to the rebellion. He was now in peaceable possession of his realm.

He went in triumph to Falaise, where he was solemnly crowned with great ceremony and parade, and all Normandy was filled with congratulations and rejoicings.

4

William's Reign in Normandy

A.D. 1040-1060

A lapse of twenty years.—Conspiracy of Guy of Burgundy.—The fool or jester.—Meetings of the conspirators.—Final plans of the conspirators.—Discovered by Galet.—Galet sets out in search of William.—He finds him asleep.—William's flight.—His narrow escape.—William is recognized.—Hubert's castle.—Hubert's sons.—Pursuit of the conspirators.—Defeat of the rebels.—Their punishment.—Curious incident.—Coats of armor.—Origin of heraldry.—Rollo de Tesson.—Keeping both oaths.—Changing sides.—Character of the ancient chieftains.—Their love of war.—Ancient castles.—Their interior construction.—Nothing respectable for the nobility but war.—Rebellions.—Insulting allusions to William's birth.—The ambuscade.—Its failure.—Insults of the garrison.—Indignation of William.—William's campaign in France.—His popularity.—William's prowess.—True nature of courage.—An ambuscade.—William's bravery.—William's victory.—Applause of the French army.—William firmly seated on his throne.—His new projects.

From the time of William's obtaining quiet possession of his realm to his invasion of England, a long period intervened. There was a lapse of more than twenty years. During this long interval, William governed his duchy, suppressed insurrections, built castles and towns, carried on wars, regulated civil institutions, and, in fact, exercised, in a very energetic and successful manner, all the functions of government—his life being diversified all the time by the usual incidents which mark the career of a great military ruler of an independent realm in the Middle Ages. We will give in this chapter a description of some of these incidents.

On one occasion a conspiracy was formed to take his life by secret assassination. A great chieftain, named Guy of Burgundy, William's uncle, was the leader of it, and a half-witted man, named Galet, who occupied the place of jester or fool in William's court, was the means of discovering and exposing it. These jesters, of whom there was always one or more in the retinue of every great prince in those days, were either very eccentric or very foolish, or half-insane men, who were dressed fantastically, in gaudy colors and with cap and bells, and were kept to make amusement for the court. The name of William's jester was Galet.

Guy of Burgundy and his fellow-conspirators occupied certain gloomy castles, built in remote and lonely situations on the confines of Normandy. Here they were accustomed to assemble for the purpose of concocting their plans, and gathering their men and their resources—doing every thing in the most cunning and secret manner. Before their scheme was fully ripe for execution, it happened that William made a hunting excursion into the neighborhood of their territory with a small band of followers—such as would be naturally got together on such a party of pleasure. Galet, the fool, was among them.

As soon as Guy and his fellow-conspirators learned that William was so near, they determined to precipitate the execution of their plan, and waylay and assassinate him on his return.

They accordingly left their secret and lonely rendezvous among the mountains one by one, in order to avoid attracting observation, and went to a town called Bayeux, through which they supposed that William would have to pass on his return. Here they held secret consultations, and formed their final plans. They sent out a part of their number, in small bands, into the region of country which William would have to cross, to occupy the various roads and passes, and thus to cut off all possibility of his escape. They made all these arrangements in the most secret and cautious manner, and began to think that they were sure of their prey.

It happened, however, that some of William's attendants, with Galet the fool among them, had preceded William on his return, and had reached Bayeux at the time when the conspirators arrived there. The townspeople did not observe the coming of the conspirators particularly, as many horsemen and soldiers were coming and going at that time, and they had no means of distinguishing the duke's friends from his enemies; but Galet, as he sauntered about the town, noticed that there were many soldiers and knights to be seen who were not of his master's party. This attracted his attention; he began to watch the motions of these strangers, and to listen, without seeming to listen, in order to catch the words they spoke to each other as they talked in groups or passed one another in the streets. He was soon satisfied that some mischief was intended. He immediately threw aside his cap and bells, and his fantastic dress, and, taking a staff in his hand, he set off on foot to go back as fast as possible in search of the duke, and give him the alarm. He found the duke at a village called Valonges. He arrived there at night. He pressed forward hastily into his master's chamber, half forcing his way through the attendants, who, accustomed to the liberties which such a personage as he was accustomed to take on all occasions, made only a feeble resistance to his wishes. He found the duke asleep, and he called upon him with a very earnest voice to awake and arise immediately, for his life was in danger.

William was at first inclined to disbelieve the story which Galet told him, and to think that there was no cause to fear. He was, however, soon convinced that Galet was right, and that there was reason for alarm. He arose and dressed himself hastily; and, inasmuch as a monarch, in the first moments of the discovery of a treasonable plot, knows not whom to trust, William wisely concluded not to trust any body. He went

WILLIAM THE CONQUEROR

himself to the stables, saddled his horse with his own hand, mounted him, and rode away. He had a very narrow escape; for, at the same time, while Galet was hastening to Valonges to give his master warning of his danger, the conspirators had been advancing to the same place, and had completely surrounded it; and they were on the eve of making an attack upon William's quarters at the very hour when he set out upon his flight. William had accordingly proceeded only a little way on his route before he heard the footsteps of galloping horses, and the clanking of arms, on the road behind him. It was a troop of the conspirators coming, who, finding that William had fled, had set off immediately in pursuit. William rode hastily into a wood, and let them go by.

William's Escape

He remained for some time in his hiding-place, and then cautiously emerged from it to continue his way. He did not dare to keep the public road, although it was night, but took a wild and circuitous route, in lanes and bypaths, which conducted him, at length, to the vicinity of the sea. Here, about day-break, he was passing a mansion, supposing that no one would observe him at so early an hour, when, suddenly, he perceived a man sitting at the gate, armed and equipped, and in an attitude of waiting. He was waiting for his horse. He was a nobleman named Hubert. He recognized William immediately as the duke, and accosted him in a tone of astonishment, saying, "Why, my lord duke, is it possible that this is you?" He was amazed to see the ruler of the realm out at such an hour, in such a condition, alone, exhausted, his dress all in disorder from the haste with which he had put it on, and his steed breathless and covered with dust, and ready, apparently, to drop down with fatigue and exhaustion.

William, finding that he was recognized, related his story. It appeared, in the end, that Hubert held his own castle and village as a tenant of one of the principal conspirators, and was bound, according to the feudal ideas of the time, to espouse his landlord's cause. He told William, however, that he had nothing to fear. "I will defend your life," said he, "as if it were my own." So saying, he called his three sons, who were all athletic and courageous young men, and commanded them to mount their horses and get ready for a march. He took William into his castle, and gave him the food and refreshment that he needed. Then he brought him again into the court-yard of the house, where William found the three young horsemen mounted and ready, and a strong and fleet steed prepared for himself. He mounted. Hubert commanded his sons to conduct the prince with all dispatch to Falaise, without traveling at all upon the highway or entering a town. They took, accordingly, a straight course across the country—which was probably then, as now, nearly destitute of inclosures—and conducted William safely to his castle at Falaise.

In the course of the morning, William's pursuers came to Hubert's castle, and asked if the duke had been seen going by. Hubert replied in the affirmative, and he mounted his steed with great readiness to go and show them the road which the fugitive had taken. He urged them to ride hard, in hopes of soon overtaking the object of their pursuit. They drove on, accordingly, with great impetuosity and ardor, under Hubert's guidance; but, as he had purposely taken a wrong road, he was only leading them further and further astray. Finally they gave up the chase, and Hubert returned with the disappointed pursuers to his fortress, William having in the mean time arrived safely at Falaise.

The conspirators now found that it was useless any longer to attempt to conceal their plans. In fact, they were already all exposed, and they knew that William would immediately summon his troops and come out to seize them. They must, therefore, either fly from the country or attempt an open rebellion. They decided on the latter—the result was a civil war. In the end, William was victorious. He took a large number of the rebels prisoners, and he adopted the following very singular plan for inflicting a suitable punishment upon them, and at the same time erecting a permanent monument of his victory. He laid out a public road across the country, on the line over which he had been conducted by the sons of Hubert, and compelled the rebels to make it. A great part of this country was low and marshy, and had been for this reason avoided by the public road, which took a circuitous course around it. The rebel prisoners were now, however, set at work to raise a terrace or embankment, on a line surveyed by William's engineers, which followed almost exactly the course of his retreat. The high road was then laid out upon this terrace, and it became immediately a public thoroughfare of great importance. It continued for several centuries one of the most frequented highways in the realm, and was known by the name of the Raised Road—*Terre levée*—throughout the kingdom. In fact, the remains of it, appearing like the ruins of an ancient rail-road embankment, exist to the present day.

In the course of the war with these rebels a curious incident occurred at one of the battles, or, rather, is said to have occurred, by the historians who tell the story, which, if true, illustrates very strikingly the romantic and chivalrous ideas of the times. Just as the battle was commencing, William perceived a strong and finely-equipped body of horsemen preparing to charge upon the very spot where he himself, surrounded by his officers, was standing. Now the armor worn by knights in battle in those times covered and concealed the figure and the face so fully, that it would have been impossible even for acquaintances and friends to recognize each other, were it not that the knights were all accustomed to wear certain devices upon some part of their armor—painted, for instance, upon their shields, or embroidered on little banners which they bore—by means of which they might be known. These devices became at length hereditary in the great families—sons being proud to wear, themselves, the emblems to which the deeds of their fathers had imparted a trace of glory and renown. The devices of different chieftains were combined, sometimes, in cases of intermarriage, or were modified in various ways; and with these minor changes they would descend from generation to generation as the family coat of arms. And this was the origin of heraldry.

Now the body of horsemen that were advancing to the charge, as above described, had each of them his device upon a little flag or banner attached to their lances. As they were advancing, William scrutinized them closely, and presently recognized in their leader a man who had formerly been upon his side. His name was Rollo de Tesson. He was one of those who had sworn fealty to him at the time when his father Robert presented him to the council, when setting out upon his pilgrimage. William accordingly exclaimed, with a loud voice, "Why, these are my friends!" The officers and the soldiers of the body-guard who were with him, taking up the cry, shouted "*Friends! friends!*" Rollo de Tesson and the other knights, who were slowly coming up, preparing to charge upon William's party, surprised at being thus accosted, paused in their advance, and finally halted. Rollo said to the other knights, who gathered around him, "I *was* his friend. I gave my oath to his father that I would stand by him and defend him with my life; and now I have this morning sworn to the Count of Cotentin"—the Count of Cotentin was the leader of the rebellion—"that I would seek out William on the battle-field, and be the first to give him a blow. I know not what to do." "Keep both oaths," replied one of his companions. "Go and strike him a gentle blow, and then defend him with your life." The whole troop seconded this proposal by acclamation. Rollo advanced, followed by the other knights, with gestures and shouts denoting that they were friends.

He rode up to William, told him that he had that morning sworn to strike him, and then dealt him a pretended blow upon his shoulder; but as both the shoulder and the hand which struck it were armed with steel, the clanking sound was all the effect that was produced. Rollo and his troop—their sworn obligation to the Count of Cotentin being thus fulfilled—turned now into the ranks of William's soldiery, and fought valiantly all day upon his side.

Although William was generally victorious in the battles that he fought, and succeeded in putting down one rebellion after another with promptness and decision, still, new rebellions and new wars were constantly breaking out, which kept his dominions in a continual state of commotion. In fact, the chieftains, the nobles, and the knights, constituting the only classes of society that exercised any influence, or were regarded with any respect in those days, were never contented except when actively employed in military campaigns. The excitements and the glory of war were the only excitements and glory that they understood, or had the means of enjoying. Their dwellings were great fortresses, built on the summits of the rocks, which, however picturesque and beautiful they appear as *ruins* now, were very gloomy and desolate as residences then. They were attractive enough when their inmates were flying to them for refuge from an enemy, or were employed within the walls in concentrating their forces and brightening up their arms for some new expedition for vengeance or plunder, but they were lonely and lifeless scenes of restlessness and discontent in times of quietness and peace.

It is difficult for us, at this day, to conceive how destitute of all the ordinary means of comfort and enjoyment, in comparison with a modern dwelling, the ancient feudal castles must have been. They were placed in situations as nearly inaccessible as possible, and the natural impediments of approach were increased by walls, and gates, and ditches, and draw-bridges. The door of access was often a window in the wall, ten or fifteen feet from the ground, to which the inmates or their friends mounted by a ladder. The floors were of stone, the walls were naked, the ceiling was a rudely-constructed series of arches. The apartments, too, were ordinarily small, and were arranged one above another, in the successive stories of a tower. Nor could these cell-like chambers be enlivened by the wide and cheerful windows of modern times, which not only admit the light to animate the scene within, but also afford to the spectator there, wide-spread, and sometimes enchanting views of the surrounding country. The castle windows of ancient days were, on the contrary, narrow loop-holes, each at the bottom of a deep recess in the thick wall. If they had been made wide they would have admitted too easily the arrows and javelins of besiegers, as well as the wind and rain of wintery storms. There were no books in these desolate dwellings, no furniture but armor, no pleasures but drinking and carousals.

Nor could these noble and valiant knights and barons occupy themselves in any useful employment. There was nothing which it was respectable for them to do but to fight. They looked down with contempt upon all the industrial pursuits of life. The cultivation of farms, the rearing of flocks and herds, arts, manufactures, and commerce—every thing of this sort, by which man can benefit his fellow-man, was entirely beneath them. In fact, their descendants to the present day, even in England, entertain the same ideas. Their younger sons can enter the army or the navy, and spend their lives in killing and destroying, or in awaiting, in idleness, dissipation, and vice, for orders to kill and destroy, without dishonor; but to engage in any way in those vast and magnificent operations of peaceful industry, on which the true greatness and glory of England depend, would be perpetual and irretrievable disgrace. A young nobleman can serve, in the most subordinate official capacity, on board a man-of-war, and take pay for it, without degradation; but to *build* a man-of-war itself and take pay for it, would be to compel his whole class to disown him.

It was in consequence of this state of feeling among the knights and barons of William's day that peace was always tedious and irksome to them, and they were never contented except when engaged in battles and campaigns. It was this feeling, probably, quite as much as any settled hostility to William's right to reign, that made his barons so eager to engage in insurrections and rebellions. There was, however, after all, a real and deep-seated opposition to William's right of succession, founded in the ideas of the day. They could not well endure that one of so humble and even ignominious birth, on the mother's side, should be the heir of so illustrious a line as the great dukes of Normandy. William's enemies were accustomed to designate him by opprobrious epithets, derived from the circumstances of his birth. Though he was patient and enduring, and often very generous in forgiving other injuries, these insults to the memory of his mother always stung him very deeply, and awakened the strongest emotions of resentment. One instance of this was so conspicuous that it is recorded in almost all the histories of William that have been written.

It was in the midst of one of the wars in which he was involved, that he was advancing across the country to the attack of a strong castle, which, in addition to the natural strength of its walls and fortifications, was defended by a numerous and powerful garrison. So confident, in fact, were the garrison in their numbers and power, that when they heard that William was advancing to attack them, they sent out a detachment to meet him. This detachment, however, were not intending to give him open battle. Their plan was to lay in ambuscade, and attack William's troops when they came to the spot, and while they were unaware of the vicinity of an enemy, and off their guard.

William, however, they found, was not off his guard. He attacked the ambuscade with so much vigor as to put the whole force immediately to flight. Of course the fugitives directed their steps toward the castle. William and his soldiers followed them in headlong pursuit. The end was, that the detachment from the garrison had scarcely time, after making good their own entrance, to raise the draw-bridges and secure the gates, so as to keep their pursuers from entering too. They did, however, succeed in doing this, and William, establishing his troops about the castle, opened his lines and commenced a regular siege.

The garrison were very naturally vexed and irritated at the bad success of their intended stratagem. To have the ambuscade not only fail of its object, but to have also the men that formed it driven thus ignominiously in, and so narrowly escaping, also, the danger of letting in the whole troop of their enemies after them, was a great disgrace. To retaliate upon William, and to throw back upon him the feelings of mortification and chagrin which they felt themselves, they mounted the walls and towers, and shouted out all sorts of reproaches and insults. Finally, when they found that they could not make mere words sufficiently stinging, they went and procured skins and hides, and aprons of leather, and every thing else that they could find that was connected with the trade of a tanner, and shook them at the troops of their assailants from the towers and walls, with shouts of merriment and derision.

William was desperately enraged at these insults. He organized an assaulting party, and by means of the great exertions which the exasperation of his men stimulated them to make, he carried some of the outworks, and took a number of prisoners. These prisoners he cut to pieces, and then caused their bloody and mangled limbs and members to be thrown, by great slings, over the castle walls.

At one time during the period which is included within the limits of this chapter, and in the course of one of those intervals of peace and quietness within his own dominions which William sometimes enjoyed, the King of France became involved in a war with one of his own rebellious subjects, and William went, with an army of Normans, to render him aid. King Henry was at first highly gratified at this prompt and effectual succor, but he soon afterward began to feel jealous of the universal popularity and renown which the young duke began soon to acquire. William was at that time only about twenty-four years old, but he took the direction of every thing—moved to and fro with the utmost celerity—planned the campaigns—directed the sieges, and by his personal accomplishments and his bravery, he won all hearts, and was the subject of every body's praises. King Henry found himself supplanted, in some measure, in the regard and honorable consideration of his subjects, and he began to feel very envious and jealous of his rival.

Sometimes particular incidents would occur, in which William's feats of prowess or dexterity would so excite the admiration of the army that he would be overwhelmed with acclamations and applause. These were generally exploits of combat on the field, or of escape from pursuers when outnumbered, in which good fortune had often, perhaps, quite as much to do in securing the result as strength or courage. But in those days a soldier's good luck was perhaps as much the subject of applause as his muscular force or his bravery; and, in fact, it was as deservedly so; for the strength of arm, and the coolness, or, rather, the ferocity of courage, which make a good combatant in personal contests on a battle-field, are qualities of brutes rather than of men. We feel a species of respect for them in the lion or tiger, but they deserve only execration when exercised in the wantonness of hatred and revenge by man against his brother man.

One of the instances of William's extraordinary success was the following. He was reconnoitering the enemy on one occasion, accompanied only by four or five knights, who acted as his attendants and body-guard. The party were at a distance from the camp of the enemy, and supposed they were not observed. They were observed, however, and immediately a party of twelve chosen horsemen was formed, and ordered to ride out and surprise them. This detachment concealed themselves in an ambuscade, at a place where the reconnoitering party must pass, and when the proper moment arrived, they burst out suddenly upon them and summoned them to surrender. Twelve against six seemed to render both flight and resistance equally vain. William, however, advanced immediately to the attack of the ambuscaders. He poised his long lance, and, riding on with it at full speed, he unhorsed and killed the foremost of them at a blow. Then, just drawing back his weapon to gather strength for another blow, he killed the second of his enemies in the same manner. His followers were so much animated at this successful onset, that they advanced very resolutely to the combat. In the mean time, the shouts carried the alarm to William's camp, and a strong party set off to rescue William and his companions. The others then turned to fly, while William followed them so eagerly and closely, that he and they who were with him overtook and disabled seven of them, and made them prisoners. The rest escaped. William and his party then turned and began to proceed toward their own camp, conveying their prisoners in their train.

They were met by King Henry himself at the head of a detachment of three hundred men, who, not knowing how much necessity there might be for efficient aid, were hastening to the scene of action. The sight of William coming home victorious, and the tales told by his companions of the invincible strength and daring which he had displayed in the sudden danger, awakened a universal enthusiasm, and the plaudits and encomiums with which the whole camp resounded were doubtless as delicious and intoxicating to him as they were bitter to the king.

It was by such deeds, and by such personal and mental characteristics as these, that William, notwithstanding the untoward influences of his birth, fought his way, during the twenty years of which we have been speaking, into general favor, and established a universal renown. He completely organized and arranged the internal affairs of his own kingdom, and established himself firmly upon the ducal throne. His mind had become mature, his resources were well developed, and his soul, always ambitious and aspiring, began to reach forward to the grasping of some grander objects of pursuit, and to the entering upon some wider field of action than his duchy of Normandy could afford. During this interval, however, he was married; and, as the circumstances of his marriage were somewhat extraordinary, we must make that event the subject of a separate chapter.

5

The Marriage

A.D. 1045-1052

Political importance of a royal marriage.—William's views in regard to his marriage.—His choice.—Matilda's genealogy.—Her relationship to William.—Matilda's accomplishments.—Her embroidery.—Matilda's industry.—The Bayeux tapestry.—The designs.—Uncouth drawing.—Preservation.—Elements of decay.—Great age of the Bayeux tapestry.—Specimens of the designs of the Bayeux tapestry.—Marriage negotiations.—Matilda's objections.—Matilda's refusal.—Her attachment to Brihtric.—Matilda's attachment not reciprocated.—Her thirst for revenge.—William and Matilda's consanguinity.—An obstacle to their marriage.—Negotiations with the pope.—Causes of delay.—William's quarrel with Matilda.—The reconciliation.—The marriage.—Rejoicings and festivities.—Residence at Rouen.—Ancient castles and palaces.—Matilda's palace.—Luxury and splendor.—Mauger, archbishop of Rouen.—William and Matilda excommunicated.—Lanfranc sent to negotiate with the pope.—His success.—Conditions of Lanfranc's treaty.—Their fulfillment.—William and Matilda's children.—Matilda's domestic character.—Objects of William's marriage.—Baldwin, Count of Flanders.—The blank letter.—Baldwin's surprise.

ONE of the most important points which an hereditary potentate has to attend to, in completing his political arrangements, is the question of his marriage. Until he has a family and an heir, men's minds are unsettled in respect to the succession, and the various rival candidates and claimants to the throne are perpetually plotting and intriguing to put themselves into a position to spring at once into his place if sickness, or a battle, or any sudden accident should take him away. This evil was more formidable than usual in the case of William, for the men who were prepared to claim his place when he was dead were all secretly or openly maintaining that their right to it was superior to his while he was living. This gave a double intensity to the excitement with which the public was perpetually agitated in respect to the crown, and kept the minds of the ambitious and the aspiring, throughout William's dominions, in a continual fever. It was obvious that a great part of the cause of this restless looking for change and consequent planning to promote it would be removed if William had a son.

It became, therefore, an important matter of state policy that the duke should be married. In fact, the barons and military chieftains who were friendly to him urged this measure upon him, on account of the great effect which they perceived it would have in settling the minds of the people of the country and consolidating his power. William accordingly began to look around for a wife. It appeared, however, in the end, that, though policy was the main consideration which first led him to contemplate marriage, love very probably exercised an important influence in determining his choice of the lady; at all events, the object of his choice was an object worthy of love. She was one of the most beautiful and accomplished princesses in Europe.

She was the daughter of a great potentate who ruled over the country of Flanders. Flanders lies upon the coast, east of Normandy, beyond the frontiers of France, and on the southern shore of the German Ocean. Her father's title was the Earl of Flanders. He governed his dominions, however, like a sovereign, and was at the head of a very effective military power. His family, too, occupied a very high rank, and enjoyed great consideration among the other princes and potentates of Europe. It had intermarried with the royal family of England, so that Matilda, the daughter of the earl, whom William was disposed to make his bride, was found, by the genealogists, who took great interest in those days in tracing such connections, to have descended in a direct line from the great English king, Alfred himself.

This relationship, by making Matilda's birth the more illustrious, operated strongly in favor of the match, as a great part of the motive which William had in view, in his intended marriage, was to aggrandize and strengthen his own position, by the connection which he was about to form. There was, however, another consanguinity in the case which had a contrary tendency. Matilda's father had been connected with the Norman as well as with the English line, and Matilda and William were in some remote sense cousins. This circumstance led, in the sequel, as will presently be seen, to serious difficulty and trouble.

Matilda was seven years younger than William. She was brought up in her father's court, and famed far and wide for her beauty and accomplishments. The accomplishments in which ladies of high rank sought to distinguish themselves in those days were two, music and embroidery. The embroidery of tapestry was the great attainment, and in this art the young Matilda acquired great skill. The tapestry which was made in the Middle Ages was used to hang against the walls of some of the more ornamented rooms in royal palaces and castles, to hide the naked surface of the stones of which the building was constructed. The cloths thus suspended were at first plain, afterward they began to be ornamented with embroidered borders or other decorations, and at length ladies learned to employ their own leisure hours, and beguile the tedium of the long confinement which many of them had to endure within their castles, in embroidering various devices and designs on the hangings intended for their own chambers, or to execute such work as presents for their friends. Matilda's industry and skill in this kind of work were celebrated far and wide.

The accomplishments which ladies take great pains to acquire in their early years are sometimes, it is said, laid almost entirely aside after their marriage; not necessarily because they are then less desirous to please, but sometimes from the abundance of domestic duty, which allows them little time, and sometimes from the pressure of their burdens of care or sorrow, which leave them no heart for the occupations of amusement or gayety. It seems not to have been so in Matilda's case, however. She resumed her needle often during the years of her wedded life, and after William had accomplished his conquest of England, she worked upon a long linen web, with immense labor, a series of designs illustrating the various events and incidents of his campaign, and the work has been preserved to the present day.

At least there is such a web now existing in the ancient town of Bayeux, in Normandy, which has been there from a period beyond the memory of men, and which tradition says was worked by Matilda. It would seem, however, that if she did it at all, she must have done it "as Solomon built the temple—with a great deal of help;" for this famous piece of embroidery, which has been celebrated among all the historians and scholars of the world for several hundred years by the name of the *Bayeux Tapestry*, is over four hundred feet long, and nearly two feet wide. The wet is of linen, while the embroidery is of woolen. It was all obviously executed with the needle, and was worked with infinite labor and care. The woolen thread which was used was of various colors, suited to represent the different objects in the design, though these colors are, of course, now much tarnished and faded.

The designs themselves are very simple and even rude, evincing very little knowledge of the principles of modern art. The specimens on the following page, of engravings made from them, will give some idea of the childish style of delineation which characterizes all Matilda's designs. Childish, however, as such a style of drawing would be considered now, it seems to have been, in Matilda's days, very much praised and admired.

PLOWING. From the Bayeux tapestry.

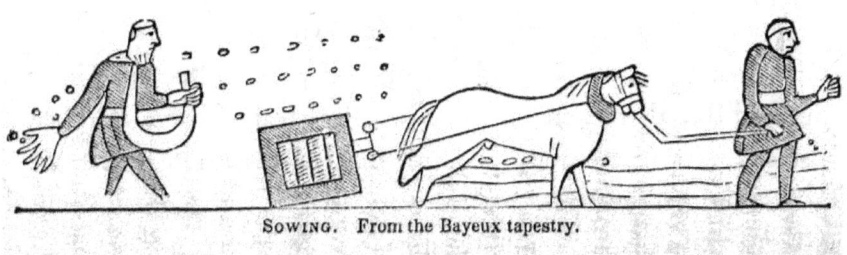
SOWING. From the Bayeux tapestry.

From the Bayeux Tapestry — Plowing and Sowing

We often have occasion to observe, in watching the course of human affairs, the frailty and transitoriness of things apparently most durable and strong. In the case of this embroidery, on the contrary, we are struck with the durability and permanence of what would seem to be most frail and fleeting. William's conquest of England took place in 1066. This piece of tapestry, therefore, if Matilda really worked it, is about eight hundred years old. And when we consider how delicate, slender, and frail is the fibre of a linen thread, and that the various elements of decay, always busy in the work of corrupting and destroying the works of man, have proved themselves powerful enough to waste away and crumble into ruin the proudest structures which he has ever attempted to rear, we are amazed that these slender filaments have been able to resist their action so long. The Bayeux tapestry has lasted nearly a thousand years. It will probably last for a thousand years to come. So that the vast and resistless power, which destroyed Babylon and Troy, and is making visible progress in the work of destroying the Pyramids, is foiled by the durability of a piece of needlework, executed by the frail and delicate fingers of a woman.

We may have occasion to advert to the Bayeux tapestry again, when we come to narrate the exploits which it was the particular object of this historical embroidery to illustrate and adorn. In the meantime, we return to our story.

The matrimonial negotiations of princes and princesses are always conducted in a formal and ceremonious manner, and through the intervention of legates, ambassadors, and commissioners without number, who are, of course, interested in protracting the proceedings, so as to prolong, as much as possible, their own diplomatic importance and power. Besides these accidental and temporary difficulties, it soon appeared that there were, in this case, some real and very formidable obstacles, which threatened for a time entirely to frustrate the scheme.

Among these difficulties there was one which was not usually, in such cases, considered of much importance, but which, in this instance, seemed for a long time to put an effectual bar to William's wishes, and that was the aversion which the young princess herself felt for the match. She could have, one would suppose, no personal feeling of repugnance against William, for he was a tall and handsome cavalier, highly graceful and accomplished, and renowned for his bravery and success in war. He was, in every respect, such a personage as would be most likely to captivate the imagination of a maiden princess in those warlike times. Matilda, however, made objections to his birth. She could not consider him as the legitimate descendant and heir of the dukes of Normandy. It is true, he was then in possession of the throne, but he was regarded by a large portion of the most powerful chieftains in his realm as a usurper. He was liable, at any time, on some sudden change of fortune, to be expelled from his dominions. His position, in a word, though for the time being very exalted, was too precarious and unstable, and his personal claims to high social rank were too equivocal, to justify her trusting her destiny in his hands. In a word, Matilda's answer to William's proposals was an absolute refusal to become his wife.

These ostensible grounds, however, on which Matilda based her refusal, plausible as they were, were not the real and true ones. The secret motive was another attachment which she had formed. There had been sent to her father's court in Flanders, from the English king, a young Saxon ambassador, whose name was Brihtric. Brihtric remained some little time at the court in Flanders, and Matilda, who saw him often at the various entertainments, celebrations, and parties of pleasure which were arranged for his amusement, conceived a strong attachment to him. He was of a very fair complexion, and his features were expressive and beautiful. He was a noble of high position in England, though, of course, his rank was inferior to that of Matilda. As it would have been deemed hardly proper for him, under the circumstances of the case, to have aspired to the princess's hand, on account of the superiority of her social position, Matilda felt that it was her duty to make known her sentiments to him, and thus to open the way. She did so; but she found, unhappy maiden, that Brihtric did not feel, himself, the love which he had inspired in her, and all the efforts and arts to which she was impelled by the instinct of affection proved wholly unavailing to call it forth. Brihtric, after fulfilling the object of his mission, took leave of Matilda coldly, while *her* heart was almost breaking, and went away.

As the sweetest wine transforms itself into the sharpest vinegar, so the warmest and most ardent love turns, when it turns at all, to the most bitter and envenomed hate. Love gave place soon in Matilda's heart to indignation, and indignation to a burning thirst for revenge. The intensity of the first excitement subsided; but Matilda never forgot and never forgave the disappointment and the indignity which she had endured. She had an opportunity long afterward to take terrible revenge on Brihtric in England, by subjecting him to cruelties and hardships there which brought him to his grave.

In the meantime, while her thoughts were so occupied with this attachment, she had, of course, no heart to listen favorably to William's proposals. Her friends would have attached no importance to the real cause of her aversion to the match, but they felt the force of the objections which could justly be advanced against William's rank, and his real right to his throne. Then the consanguinity of the parties was a great source of embarrassment and trouble. Persons as nearly related to each other as they were, were forbidden by the Roman Catholic rules to marry. There was such a thing as getting a dispensation from the pope, by which the marriage would be authorized. William accordingly sent ambassadors to Rome to negotiate this business. This, of course, opened a new field for difficulties and delays.

The papal authorities were accustomed, in such cases, to exact as the price, or, rather, as the condition of their dispensation, some grant or beneficial conveyance from the parties interested, to the Church, such as the foundation of an abbey or a monastery, the building of a chapel, or the endowment of a charity, by way as it were, of making amends to the Church, by the benefit thus received, for whatever injury the cause of religion and morality might sustain by the relaxation of a divine law. Of course, this being the end in view, the tendency on the part of the authorities at Rome would be to protract the negotiations, so as to obtain from the suitor's impatience better terms in the end. The ambassadors and commissioners, too, on William's part, would have no strong motive for hastening the proceedings. Rome was an agreeable place of residence, and to live there as the ambassador of a royal duke of Normandy was to enjoy a high degree of consideration, and to be surrounded continually by scenes of magnificence and splendor. Then, again, William himself was not always at leisure to urge the business forward by giving it his own close attention; for, during the period while these negotiations were pending, he was occupied, from time to time, with foreign wars, or in the suppression of rebellions among his barons. Thus, from one cause and another, it seemed as if the business would never come to an end.

In fact, a less resolute and determined man than William would have given up in despair, for it was seven years, it is said, before the affair was brought to a conclusion. One story is told of the impetuous energy which William manifested in this suit, which seems almost incredible.

It was after the negotiations had been protracted for several years, and at a time when the difficulties were principally those arising from

Matilda's opposition, that the occurrence took place. It was at an interview which William had with Matilda in the streets of Bruges, one of her father's cities. All that took place at the interview is not known, but in the end of it William's resentment at Matilda's treatment of him lost all bounds. He struck her or pushed her so violently as to throw her down upon the ground. It is said that he struck her repeatedly, and then, leaving her with her clothes all soiled and disheveled, rode off in a rage. Love quarrels are often the means of bringing the contending parties nearer together than they were before, but such a terrible love quarrel as this, we hope, is very rare.

Violent as it was, however, it was followed by a perfect reconciliation, and in the end all obstacles were removed, and William and Matilda were married. The event took place in 1052.

The marriage ceremony was performed at one of William's castles, on the frontiers of Normandy, as it is customary for princes and kings to be married always in their own dominions. Matilda was conducted there with great pomp and parade by her parents, and was accompanied by a large train of attendants and friends. This company, mounted—both knights and ladies—on horses beautifully caparisoned, moved across the country like a little army on a march, or rather like a triumphal procession escorting a queen. Matilda was received at the castle with distinguished honor, and the marriage celebrations, and the entertainments accompanying it, were continued for several days. It was a scene of unusual festivity and rejoicing.

The dress both of William and Matilda, on this occasion, was very specially splendid. She wore a mantle studded with the most costly jewels; and, in addition to the other splendors of his dress, William too wore a mantle and a helmet, both of which were richly adorned with the same costly decorations. So much importance was attached, in those days, to this outward show, and so great was the public interest taken in it, that these dresses of William and Matilda, with all the jewelry that adorned them, were deposited afterward in the great church at Bayeux, where they remained a sort of public spectacle, the property of the Church, for nearly five hundred years.

From the castle of Augi, where the marriage ceremonies were performed, William proceeded, after these first festivities and rejoicings were over, to the great city of Rouen, conducting his bride thither with great pomp and parade. Here the young couple established themselves, living in the enjoyment of every species of luxury and splendor which were attainable in those days. As has already been said, the interiors, even of royal castles and palaces, presented but few of the comforts and conveniences deemed essential to the happiness of a home in modern times. The European ladies of the present day delight in their suites of retired and well-furnished apartments, adorned with velvet carpets, and silken curtains, and luxuriant beds of down, with sofas and couches adapted to every fancy which the caprice of fatigue or restlessness may assume, and cabinets stored with treasures, and libraries of embellished books—the whole scene illuminated by the splendor of gas-lights, whose brilliancy is reflected by mirrors and candelabras, sparkling with a thousand hues. Matilda's feudal palace presented no such scenes as these. The cold stone floors were covered with mats of rushes. The walls —if the naked masonry was hidden at all—were screened by hangings of coarse tapestry, ornamented with uncouth and hideous figures. The beds were miserable pallets, the windows were loopholes, and the castle itself had all the architectural characteristics of a prison.

Still, there was a species of luxury and splendor even then. Matilda had splendid horses to ride, all magnificently caparisoned. She had dresses adorned most lavishly with gold and jewels. There were troops of valiant knights, all glittering in armor of steel, to escort her on her journeys, and accompany and wait upon her on her excursions of pleasure; and there were grand banquets and carousals, from time to time, in the long castle hall, with tournaments, and races, and games, and other military shows, conducted with great parade and pageantry. Matilda thus commenced her married life in luxury and splendor.

In luxury and splendor, but not in peace. William had an uncle, whose name was Mauger. He was the Archbishop of Rouen, and was a dignitary of great influence and power. Now it was, of course, the interest of William's relatives that he should not be married, as every increase of probability that his crown would descend to direct heirs diminished their future chances of the succession, and of course undermined their present importance. Mauger had been very much opposed to this match, and had exerted himself in every way, while the negotiations were pending, to impede and delay them. The point which he most strenuously urged was the consanguinity of the parties, a point to which it was incumbent on him, as he maintained—being the head of the Church in Normandy—particularly to attend. It seems that, notwithstanding William's negotiations with the pope to obtain a dispensation, the affair was not fully settled at Rome before the marriage; and very soon after the celebration of the nuptials, Mauger fulminated an edict of excommunication against both William and Matilda, for intermarrying within the degrees of relationship which the canons of the Church proscribed.

An excommunication, in the Middle Ages, was a terrible calamity. The person thus condemned was made, so far as such a sentence could effect it, an outcast from man, and a wretch accursed of Heaven. The most terrible denunciations were uttered against him, and in the case of a prince, like that of William, his subjects were all absolved from their allegiance, and forbidden to succor or defend him. A powerful potentate like William could maintain himself for a time against the influence and effects of such a course, but it was pretty sure to work more and more strongly against him through the superstitions of the people, and to wear him out in the end.

William resolved to appeal at once to the pope, and to effect, by some means or other, the object of securing his dispensation. There was a certain monk, then obscure and unknown, but who afterward became a very celebrated public character, named Lanfranc, whom, for some reason or other, William supposed to possess the necessary qualifications for this mission. He accordingly gave him his instructions and sent him away. Lanfranc proceeded to Rome, and there he managed the negotiation with the pope so dexterously as soon to bring it to a conclusion.

The arrangement which he made was this. The pope was to grant the dispensation and confirm the marriage, thus removing the sentence of excommunication which the Archbishop Mauger had pronounced, on condition that William should build and endow a hospital for a hundred poor persons, and also erect two abbeys, one to be built by himself, for monks, and one by Matilda, for nuns. Lanfranc agreed to these conditions on the part of William and Matilda, and they, when they came to be informed of them, accepted and confirmed them with great joy. The ban of excommunication was removed; all Normandy acquiesced in the marriage, and William and Matilda proceeded to form the plans and to superintend the construction of the abbeys.

They selected the city of Caen for the site. The place of this city will be seen marked upon the map near the northern coast of Normandy. It was situated in a broad and pleasant valley, at the confluence of two rivers, and was surrounded by beautiful and fertile meadows. It was strongly fortified, being surrounded by walls and towers, which William's ancestors, the dukes of Normandy, had built. William and Matilda took a strong interest in the plans and constructions connected with the building of the abbeys. William's was a very extensive edifice, and contained within its enclosures a royal palace for himself, where, in subsequent years, himself and Matilda often resided.

The principal buildings of these abbeys still stand, though the walls and fortifications of Caen are gone. The buildings are used now for other purposes than those for which they were erected, but they retain the names originally given them, and are visited by great numbers of tourists, being regarded with great interest as singular memorials of the past—twin monuments commemorating an ancient marriage.

The marriage being thus finally confirmed and acquiesced in, William and Matilda enjoyed a long period of domestic peace. The oldest child was a son. He was born within a year of the marriage, and William named him Robert, that, as the reader will recollect, having been the name of William's father. There was, in process of time, a large family of children. Their names were Robert, William Rufus, Henry, Cecilia, Agatha, Constance, Adela, Adelaide, and Gundred. Matilda devoted herself with great maternal fidelity to the care and education of these children, and many of them became subsequently historical personages of the highest distinction.

The object which, it will be recollected, was one of William's main inducements for contracting this alliance, namely, the strengthening of his power by thus connecting himself with the reigning family of Flanders, was, in a great measure, accomplished. The two governments, leagued together by this natural tie, strengthened each other's power, and often rendered each other essential assistance, though there was one occasion, subsequently, when William's reliance on this aid was disappointed. It was as follows:

When he was planning his invasion of England, he sent to Matilda's brother, Baldwin, who was then Count of Flanders, inviting him to raise a force and join him. Baldwin, who considered the enterprise as dangerous and Quixotic, sent back word to inquire what share of the English territory William would give him if he would go and help him conquer it. William thought that this attempt to make a bargain beforehand, for a division of spoil, evinced a very mercenary and distrustful spirit on the part of his brother-in-law—a spirit which he was not at all disposed to encourage. He accordingly took a sheet of parchment, and writing nothing within, he folded it in the form of a letter, and wrote upon the outside the following rhyme:

"Beau frère, en Angleterre vous aures
Ce qui dedans escript, vous trouveres."

Which royal distich might be translated thus:

> "Your share, good brother, of the land we win,
> You'll find entitled and described within."

William forwarded the empty missive by the hand of a messenger, who delivered it to Baldwin as if it were a dispatch of great consequence. Baldwin received it eagerly and opened it at once. He was surprised at finding nothing within; and after turning the parchment every way, in vain search after the description of his share, he asked the messenger what it meant. "It means," said he, "that as there is nothing writ within, so nothing you shall have."

Notwithstanding this witticism, however, some arrangement seems afterward to have been made between the parties, for Flanders did, in fact, contribute an important share toward the force which William raised when preparing for the invasion.

6

The Lady Emma

A.D. 1002-1052

William's claims to the English throne.—The Lady Emma.—Claimants to the English throne.—Ethelred.—Ethelred subdued.—He flies to Normandy.—Massacre of the Danes.—Horrors of civil war.—Ethelred's tyranny.—Emma's policy.—Emma's humiliation.—Ethelred invited to return.—Restoration of Ethelred and Emma.—War with Canute.—Ethelred's death.—Situation of Emma.—Her children.—War with Canute.—Treaty between Edmund and Canute.—Death of Edmund.—Accession of Canute.—Canute's wise policy.—His treatment of Edmund's children.—Canute marries Emma.—Opposition of her sons.—Emma again queen of England.—The Earl Godwin.—Canute's death.—He bequeaths the kingdom to Harold.—Emma's plots for her children.—Her letter to them.—Disastrous issue of Alfred's expedition.—His terrible sentence.—Edward's accession.—Emma wretched and miserable.—Accusations against Emma.—Her wretched end.—Edmund's children.—Godwin.—Harold.—Plans of Edward.—Plots and counterplots.

IT is not to be supposed that, even in the warlike times of which we are writing, such a potentate as a duke of Normandy would invade a country like England, so large and powerful in comparison to his own, without some pretext. William's pretext was, that he himself was the legitimate successor to the English crown, and that the English king who possessed it at the time of his invasion was a usurper. In order that the reader may understand the nature and origin of this his claim, it is necessary to relate somewhat in full the story of the Lady Emma.

By referring to the genealogy of the Norman line of dukes contained in the second chapter of this volume, it will be seen that Emma was the daughter of the first Richard. She was celebrated in her early years for her great personal beauty. They called her *the Pearl of Normandy*.

She married, at length, one of the kings of England, whose name was Ethelred. England was at that time distracted by civil wars, waged between the two antagonist races of Saxons and Danes. There were, in fact, two separate dynasties or lines of kings, who were contending, all the time, for the mastery. In these contests, sometimes the Danes would triumph for a time, and sometimes the Saxons; and sometimes both races would have a royal representative in the field, each claiming the throne, and reigning over separate portions of the island. Thus there were, at certain periods, two kingdoms in England, both covering the same territory, and claiming the government of the same population—with two kings, two capitals, two administrations—while the wretched inhabitants were distracted and ruined by the terrible conflicts to which these hostile pretensions gave rise.

Ethelred was of the Saxon line. He was a widower at the time of his marriage to Emma, nearly forty years old, and he had, among other children by his former wife, a son named Edmund, an active, energetic young man, who afterward became king. One motive which he had in view in marrying Emma was to strengthen his position by securing the alliance of the Normans of Normandy. The Danes, his English enemies, were Normans. The government of Normandy would therefore be naturally inclined to take part with them. By this marriage, however, Ethelred hoped to detach the Normans of France from the cause of his enemies, and to unite them to his own. He would thus gain a double advantage, strengthening himself by an accession which weakened his foes.

His plan succeeded so far as inducing Richard himself, the Duke of Normandy, to espouse his cause, but it did not enable Ethelred to triumph over his enemies. They, on the contrary, conquered *him*, and, in the end, drove him from the country altogether. He fled to Normandy for refuge, with Emma his wife, and his two young sons. Their names were Edward and Alfred.

Richard II., Emma's brother, who was then the Duke of Normandy, received the unhappy fugitives with great kindness, although *he*, at least, scarcely deserved it. It was not surprising that he was driven from his native realm, for he possessed none of those high qualities of mind which fit men to conquer or to govern. Like all other weak-minded tyrants, he substituted cruelty for wisdom and energy in his attempts to subjugate his foes. As soon as he was married to Emma, for instance, feeling elated and strong at the great accession of power which he imagined he had obtained by this alliance, he planned a general massacre of the Danes, and executed it on a given day, by means of private orders, sent secretly throughout the kingdom. Vast numbers of the Danes were destroyed; and so great was the hatred of the two races for each other, that they who had these bloody orders to obey executed them with a savage cruelty that was absolutely horrible. In one instance they buried women to the waist, and then set dogs upon them, to tear their naked flesh until they died in agony. It would be best, in narrating history, to suppress such horrid details as these, were it not that in a land like this, where so much depends upon the influence of every individual in determining whether the questions and discussions which are from time to time arising, and are hereafter to arise, shall be settled peacefully, or by a resort to violence and civil war, it is very important that we should all know what civil war is, and to what horrible atrocities it inevitably leads.

Alfred the Great, when he was contending with the Danes in England, a century before this time, treated them, so far as he gained advantages over them, with generosity and kindness; and this policy wholly conquered them in the end. Ethelred, on the other hand, tried the effect of the most tyrannical cruelty, and the effect was only to arouse his enemies to a more determined and desperate resistance. It was the phrensy of vengeance and hate that these atrocities awakened every where among the Danes, which nerved them with so much vigor and strength that they finally expelled him from the island; so that, when he arrived in Normandy, a fugitive and an exile, he came in the character of a dethroned tyrant, execrated for his senseless and atrocious cruelties, and not in that of an unhappy prince driven from his home by the pressure of unavoidable calamity. Nevertheless, Richard, the Duke of Normandy, received him, as we have already said, with kindness. He felt the obligation of receiving the exiled monarch in a hospitable manner, if not on his own account, at least for the sake of Emma and the children.

The origin and end of Emma's interest in Ethelred seems to have been merely ambition. The "Pearl of Normandy" had given herself to this monster for the sake, apparently, of the glory of being the English queen. Her subsequent conduct compels the readers of history to make this supposition, which otherwise would be uncharitable. She now mourned her disappointment in finding that, instead of being sustained by her husband in the lofty position to which she aspired, she was obliged to come back to her former home again, to be once more dependent, and with the additional burden of her husband himself, and her children, upon her father's family. Her situation was rendered even still more humiliating, in some degree, by the circumstances that her father was no longer alive, and that it was to her brother, on whom her natural claim was far less strong, that she had now to look for shelter and protection. Richard, however, received them all in a kind and generous manner.

In the mean time, the wars and commotions which had driven Ethelred away continued to rage in England, the Saxons gradually gaining ground against the Danes. At length the king of the Danes, who had seized the government when Ethelred was expelled, died. The Saxons then regained their former power, and they sent commissioners to Ethelred to propose his return to England. At the same time, they expressed their unwillingness to receive him, unless they could bind him, by a solemn treaty, to take a very different course of conduct, in the future management of his government, from that which he had pursued before. Ethelred and Emma were eager to regain, on any terms, their lost throne. They sent over ambassadors empowered to make, in Ethelred's name, any promises which the English nobles might demand; and shortly afterward the royal pair crossed the Channel and went to London, and Ethelred was acknowledged there by the *Saxon* portion of the population of the island once more as king.

The *Danes*, however, though weakened, were not yet disposed to submit. They declared their allegiance to *Canute*, who was the successor in the *Danish* line. Then followed a long war between Canute and Ethelred. Canute was a man of extraordinary sagacity and intelligence, and also of great courage and energy. Ethelred, on the other hand, proved himself, notwithstanding all his promises, incurably inefficient, cowardly, and cruel. In fact, his son Prince Edmund, the son of his first wife, was far more efficient than his father in resisting Canute and the Danes. Edmund was active and fearless, and he soon acquired very extensive power. In fact, he seems to have held the authority of his father in very little respect. One striking instance of this insubordination occurred. Ethelred had taken offense, for some reason or other, at one of the nobles in his realm, and had put him to death, and confiscated his estates; and, in addition to this, with a cruelty characteristic of him, he shut up the unhappy widow of his victim, a young and beautiful woman, in a gloomy convent, as a prisoner. Edmund, his son, went to the convent, liberated the prisoner, and made her his own wife.

JACOB ABBOTT

The Rescue

With such unfriendly relations between the king and his son, who seems to have been the ablest general in his father's army, there could be little hope of making head against such an enemy as Canute the Dane. In fact, the course of public affairs went on from bad to worse, Emma leading all the time a life of unceasing anxiety and alarm. At length, in 1016, Ethelred died, and Emma's cup of disappointment and humiliation was now full. Her own sons, Edward and Alfred, had no claims to the crown; for Edmund, being the son by a former marriage, was older than they. They were too young to take personally an active part in the fierce contests of the day, and thus fight their way to importance and power. And then Edmund, who was now to become king, would, of course, feel no interest in advancing *them*, or doing honor to *her*. A son who would thwart and counteract the plans and measures of a father, as Edmund had done, would be little likely to evince much deference or regard for a mother-in-law, or for half-brothers, whom he would naturally consider as his rivals. In a word, Emma had reason to be alarmed at the situation of insignificance and danger in which she found herself suddenly placed. She fled a second time, in destitution and distress, to her brother's in Normandy. She was now, however, a widow, and her children were fatherless. It is difficult to decide whether to consider her situation as better or worse on this account, than it was at her former exile.

Her sons were lads, but little advanced beyond the period of childhood; and Edward, the eldest, on whom the duty of making exertions to advance the family interests would first devolve, was of a quiet and gentle spirit, giving little promise that he would soon be disposed to enter vigorously upon military campaigns. Edmund, on the other hand, who was now king, was in the prime of life, and was a man of great spirit and energy. There was a reasonable prospect that he would live many years; and even if he were to be suddenly cut off, there seemed to be no hope of the restoration of Emma to importance or power; for Edmund was married and had two sons, one of whom would be entitled to succeed him in case of his decease. It seemed, therefore, to be Emma's destiny now, to spend the remainder of her days with her children in neglect and obscurity. The case resulted differently, however, as we shall see in the end.

Edmund, notwithstanding his prospect of a long and prosperous career, was cut off suddenly, after a stormy reign of one year. During his reign, Canute the Dane had been fast gaining ground in England, notwithstanding the vigor and energy with which Edmund had opposed him. Finally, the two monarchs assembled their armies, and were about to fight a great final battle. Edmund sent a flag of truce to Canute's camp, proposing that, to save the effusion of blood, they should agree to decide the case by single combat, and that he and Canute should be the champions, and fight in presence of the armies. Canute declined this proposal. He was himself small and slender in form, while Edmund was distinguished for his personal development and muscular strength. Canute therefore declined the personal contest, but offered to leave the question to the decision of a council chosen from among the leading nobles on either side. This plan was finally adopted. The council convened, and, after long deliberations, they framed a treaty by which the country was divided between the two potentates, and a sort of peace was restored. A very short period after this treaty was settled, Edmund was murdered.

Canute immediately laid claim to the whole realm. He maintained that it was a part of the treaty that the partition of the kingdom was to continue only during their joint lives, and that, on the death of either, the whole was to pass to the survivor of them. The Saxon leaders did not admit this, but they were in no condition very strenuously to oppose it. Ethelred's sons by Emma were too young to come forward as leaders yet; and as to Edmund's, they were mere children. There was, therefore, no one whom they could produce as an efficient representative of the Saxon line, and thus the Saxons were compelled to submit to Canute's pretensions, at least for a time. They would not wholly give up the claims of Edmund's children, but they consented to waive them for a season. They gave Canute the guardianship of the boys until they should become of age, and allowed him, in the mean time, to reign, himself, over the whole land.

Canute exercised his power in a very discreet and judicious manner, seeming intent, in all his arrangements, to protect the rights and interests of the Saxons as well as of the Danes. It might be supposed that the lives of the young Saxon princes, Edmund's sons, would not have been safe in his hands; but the policy which he immediately resolved to pursue was to conciliate the Saxons, and not to intimidate and coerce them. He therefore did the young children no harm, but sent them away out of the country to Denmark, that they might, if possible, be gradually forgotten. Perhaps he thought that, if the necessity should arise for it, they might there, at any time, be put secretly to death.

There was another reason still to prevent Canute's destroying these children, which was, that if *they* were removed, the claims of the Saxon line would not thereby be extinguished, but would only be transferred to Emma's children in Normandy, who, being older, were likely the sooner to be in a condition to give him trouble as rivals. It was therefore a very wise and sagacious policy which prompted him to keep the young children of Edmund alive, but to remove them to a safe distance out of the way.

In respect to Emma's children, Canute conceived a different plan for guarding against any danger which came from their claims, and that was, to propose to take their mother for his wife. By this plan her family would come into his power, and then her own influence and that of her Norman friends would be forever prevented from taking sides against him. He accordingly made the proposal. Emma was ambitious enough of again returning to her former position of greatness as English queen to accept it eagerly. The world condemned her for being so ready to marry, for her second husband, the deadly enemy and rival of the first; but it was all one to her whether her husband was Saxon or Dane, provided that she could be queen.

The boys, or, rather, the young men, for they were now advancing to maturity, were very strongly opposed to this connection. They did all in their power to prevent its consummation, and they never forgave their mother for thus basely betraying their interests. They were the more incensed at this transaction, because it was stipulated in the marriage articles between Canute and Emma that their *future* children—the offspring of the marriage then contracted—should succeed to the throne of England, to the exclusion of all previously born on either side. Thus Canute fancied that he had secured his title, and that of his descendants, to the crown forever, and Emma prepared to return to England as once more its queen. The marriage was celebrated with great pomp and splendor, and Emma, bidding Normandy and her now alienated children farewell, was conducted in state to the royal palace in London.

We must now pass over, with a very few words, a long interval of twenty years. It was the period of Canute's reign, which was prosperous and peaceful. During this period Emma's Norman sons continued in Normandy. She had another son in England a few years after her marriage, who was named Canute, after his father, but he is generally known in history by the name of Hardicanute, the prefix being a Saxon word denoting energetic or strong. Canute had also a very celebrated minister in his government named Godwin. Godwin was a Saxon of a very humble origin, and the history of his life constitutes quite a romantic tale. [It is given at length in the last chapter of our history of Alfred the Great.] He was a man of extraordinary talents and character, and at the time of Canute's death he was altogether the most powerful subject in the realm.

When Canute found that he was about to die, and began to consider what arrangements he should make for the succession, he concluded that it would not be safe for him to fulfill the agreement made in his marriage contract with Emma, that the children of that marriage should inherit the kingdom; for Hardicanute, who was entitled to succeed under that covenant, was only about sixteen or seventeen years old, and consequently too young to attempt to govern. He therefore made a will, in which he left the kingdom to an older son, named Harold—a son whom he had had before his marriage with Emma. This was the signal for a new struggle. The influence of the Saxons and of Emma's friends was of course in favor of Hardicanute, while the Danes espoused the cause of Harold. Godwin at length taking sides with this last-named party, Harold was established on the throne, and Emma and all her children, whether descended from Ethelred or Canute, were set aside and forgotten.

Emma was not at all disposed to acquiesce in this change of fortune. She remained in England, but was secretly incensed at her second husband's breach of faith toward her; and as he had abandoned the child of his marriage with her for *his* former children, she now determined to abandon him for *hers*. She gave up Hardicanute's cause, therefore, and began secretly to plot among the Saxon population for bringing forward her son Edward to the throne. When she thought that things were ripe for the execution of the plot, she wrote a letter to her children in Normandy, saying to them that the Saxon population were weary of the Danish line, and were ready, she believed, to rise in behalf of the ancient Saxon line, if the true representative of it would appear to lead them. She therefore invited them to come to London and consult with her on the subject. She directed them, however, to come, if they came at all, in a quiet and peaceful manner, and without any appearance of hostile intent, inasmuch as any thing which might seem like a foreign invasion would awaken universal jealousy and alarm.

When this letter was received by the brothers in Normandy, the eldest, Edward, declined to go, but gave his consent that Alfred should undertake the expedition if he were disposed. Alfred accepted the proposal. In fact, the temperament and character of the two brothers were very different. Edward was sedate, serious, and timid. Alfred was ardent and aspiring. The younger, therefore, decided to take the risk of crossing the Channel, while the elder preferred to remain at home.

The result was very disastrous. Contrary to his mother's instructions, Alfred took with him quite a troop of Norman soldiers. He crossed the Channel in safety, and advanced across the country some distance toward London. Harold sent out a force to intercept him. He was surrounded, and he himself and all his followers were taken prisoners. He was sentenced to lose his eyes, and he died in a few days after the execution of this terrible sentence, from the mingled effects of fever and of mental anguish and despair. Emma fled to Flanders.

Finally Harold died, and Hardicanute succeeded him. In a short time Hardicanute died, leaving no heirs, and now, of course, there was no one left [The children of Ethelred's oldest son, Edmund, were in Hungary at this time, and seem to have been wellnigh forgotten] to compete with Emma's oldest son Edward, who had remained all this time quietly in Normandy. He was accordingly proclaimed king. This was in 1041. He reigned for twenty years, having commenced his reign about the time that William the Conqueror was established in the possession of his dominions as Duke of Normandy. Edward had known William intimately during his long residence in Normandy, and William came to visit him in England in the course of his reign. William, in fact, considered himself as Edward's heir; for as Edward, though married, had no children, the dukes of the Norman line were his nearest relatives. He obtained, he said, a promise from Edward that Edward would sanction and confirm his claim to the English crown, in the event of his decease, by bequeathing it to William in his will.

Emma was now advanced in years. The ambition which had been the ruling principle of her life would seem to have been well satisfied, so far as it is possible to satisfy ambition, for she had had two husbands and two sons, all kings of England. But as she advanced toward the close of her career, she found herself wretched and miserable. Her son Edward could not forgive her for her abandonment of himself and his brother, to marry a man who was their own and their father's bitterest enemy. She had made a formal treaty in her marriage covenant to exclude them from the throne. She had treated them with neglect during all the time of Canute's reign, while she was living with him in London in power and splendor. Edward accused her, also, of having connived at his brother Alfred's death. The story is, that he caused her to be tried on this charge by the ordeal of fire. This method consisted of laying red-hot irons upon the stone floor of a church, at certain distances from each other, and requiring the accused to walk over them with naked feet. If the accused was innocent, Providence, as they supposed, would so guide his footsteps that he should not touch the irons. Thus, if he was innocent, he would go over safely; if guilty, he would be burned. Emma, according to the story of the times, was subjected to this test, in the Cathedral of Winchester, to determine whether she was cognizant of the murder of her son. Whether this is true or not, there is no doubt that Edward confined her a prisoner in the monastery at Winchester, where she ended her days at last in neglect and wretchedness.

When Edward himself drew near to the close of his life, his mind was greatly perplexed in respect to the succession. There was one descendant of his brother Edmund—whose children, it will be remembered, Canute had sent away to Denmark, in order to remove them out of the way—who was still living in Hungary. The name of this descendant was Edward. He was, in fact, the lawful heir to the crown. But he had spent his life in foreign countries, and was now far away; and, in the mean time, the Earl Godwin, who has been already mentioned as the great

Saxon nobleman who rose from a very humble rank to the position of the most powerful subject in the realm, obtained such an influence, and wielded so great a power, that he seemed at one time stronger than the king himself. Godwin at length died, but his son Harold, who was as energetic and active as his father, inherited his power, and seemed, as Edward thought, to be aspiring to the future possession of the throne. Edward had hated Godwin and all his family, and was now extremely anxious to prevent the possibility of Harold's accession. He accordingly sent to Hungary to bring Edward, his nephew, home. Edward came, bringing his family with him. He had a young son named Edgar. It was King Edward's plan to make arrangements for bringing this Prince Edward to the throne after his death, that Harold might be excluded.

The plan was a very judicious one, but it was unfortunately frustrated by Prince Edward's death, which event took place soon after he arrived in England. The young Edgar, then a child, was, of course, his heir. The king was convinced that no government which could be organized in the name of Edgar would be able to resist the mighty power of Harold, and he turned his thoughts, therefore, again to the accession of William of Normandy, who was the nearest relative on his mother's side, as the only means of saving the realm from falling into the hands of the usurper Harold. A long and vexatious contest then ensued, in which the leading powers and influences of the kingdom were divided and distracted by the plans, plots, maneuvers, and counter maneuvers of Harold to obtain the accession for himself, and of Edward to secure it for William of Normandy. In this contest Harold conquered in the first instance, and Edward and William in the end.

7

King Harold

A.D. 1063-1066

Harold and William.—Quarrel between Godwin and Edward.—Treaty between Godwin and Edward.—Hostages.—The giving of hostages now abandoned.—Cruelties inflicted.—Canute's hostages.—Godwin's hostages.—Edward declines to give up the hostages.—Harold goes to Normandy.—Harold's interview with Edward.—The storm.—Harold shipwrecked.—Guy, count of Ponthieu.—Harold a prisoner.—He is ransomed by William.—William's hospitality.—His policy in this.—William's treatment of his guests.—William's policy.—William makes known to Harold his claims to the English crown.—Harold's dissimulation.—William's precautions.—The betrothment.—William retains a hostage.—Harold's apparent acquiescence.—The public oath.—The great assembly of knights and nobles.—The threefold oath.—William's precaution.—The sacred relics.—Harold's departure.—His measures to secure the throne.—Age and infirmities of Edward.—Westminster.—Edward's death.—The crown offered to Harold.—Harold's coronation.—He knights Edgar.—Harold violates his plighted faith to William.

HAROLD, the son of the Earl Godwin, who was maneuvering to gain possession of the English throne, and William of Normandy, though they lived on opposite sides of the English Channel, the one in

France and the other in England, were still personally known to each other; for not only had William, as was stated in the last chapter, paid a visit to England, but Harold himself, on one occasion, made an excursion to Normandy. The circumstances of this expedition were, in some respects, quite extraordinary, and illustrate in a striking manner some of the peculiar ideas and customs of the times. They were as follows:

During the life of Harold's father Godwin, there was a very serious quarrel between him, that is, Godwin, and King Edward, in which both the king and his rebellious subject marshaled their forces, and for a time waged against each other an open and sanguinary war. In this contest the power of Godwin had proved so formidable, and the military forces which he succeeded in marshaling under his banners were so great, that Edward's government was unable effectually to put him down. At length, after a long and terrible struggle, which involved a large part of the country in the horrors of a civil war, the belligerents made a treaty with each other, which settled their quarrel by a sort of compromise. Godwin was to retain his high position and rank as a subject, and to continue in the government of certain portions of the island which had long been under his jurisdiction; he, on his part, promising to dismiss his armies, and to make war upon the king no more. He bound himself to the faithful performance of these covenants by giving the king *hostages*.

The hostages given up on such occasions were always near and dear relatives and friends, and the understanding was, that if the party giving them failed in fulfilling his obligations, the innocent and helpless hostages were to be entirely at the mercy of the other party into whose custody they had been given. The latter would, in such cases, imprison them, torture them, or put them to death, with a greater or less degree of severity in respect to the infliction of pain, according to the degree of exasperation which the real or fancied injury which he had received awakened in his mind.

This cruel method of binding fierce and unprincipled men to the performance of their promises has been universally abandoned in modern times, though in the rude and early stages of civilization it has been practiced among all nations, ancient and modern. The hostages chosen were often of young and tender years, and were always such as to render the separation which took place when they were torn from their friends most painful, as it was the very object of the selection to obtain those who were most beloved. They were delivered into the hands of those whom they had always regarded as their bitterest enemies, and who, of course, were objects of aversion and terror. They were sent away into places of confinement and seclusion, and kept in the custody of strangers, where they lived in perpetual fear that some new outbreak between the contending parties would occur, and consign them to torture or death. The cruelties sometimes inflicted, in such cases, on the innocent hostages, were awful. At one time, during the contentions between Ethelred and Canute, Canute, being driven across the country to the sea-coast, and there compelled to embark on board his ships to make his escape, was cruel enough to cut off the hands and the feet of some hostages which Ethelred had previously given him, and leave them writhing in agony on the sands of the shore.

The hostages which are particularly named by historians as given by Godwin to King Edward were his son and his grandson. Their names were Ulnoth and Hacune. Ulnoth, of course, was Harold's brother, and Hacune his nephew. Edward, thinking that Godwin would contrive some means of getting these securities back into his possession again if he attempted to keep them in England, decided to send them to Normandy, and to put them under the charge of William the duke for safe keeping. When Godwin died, Harold applied to Edward to give up the hostages, since, as he alleged, there was no longer any reason for detaining them. They had been given as security for *Godwin's* good behavior, and now Godwin was no more.

Edward could not well refuse to surrender them, and yet, as Harold succeeded to the power, and evidently possessed all the ambition of his father, it seemed to be, politically, as necessary to retain the hostages now as it had been before. Edward, therefore, without absolutely refusing to surrender them, postponed and evaded compliance with Harold's demand, on the ground that the hostages were in Normandy. He was going, he said, to send for them as soon as he could make the necessary arrangements for bringing them home in safety.

Under these circumstances, Harold determined to go and bring them himself. He proposed this plan to Edward. Edward would not absolutely refuse his consent, but he did all in his power to discourage such an expedition. He told Harold that William of Normandy was a crafty and powerful man; that by going into his dominions he would put himself entirely into his power, and would be certain to involve himself in some serious difficulty. This interview between Harold and the king is commemorated on the Bayeux tapestry by the opposite uncouth design.

What effect Edward's disapproval of the project produced upon Harold's mind is not certainly known. It is true that he went across the Channel, but the accounts of the crossing are confused and contradictory, some of them stating that, while sailing for pleasure with a party of attendants and companions on the coast, he was blown off from the shore and driven across to France by a storm. The probability, however, is, that this story was only a pretense. He was determined to go, but not wishing to act openly in defiance of the king's wishes, he contrived to be blown off, in order to make it seem that he went against his will.

At all events, the *storm* was real, whether his being compelled to leave the English shores by the power of it was real or pretended. It carried him, too, out of his course, driving him up the Channel to the eastward of Normandy, where he had intended to land, and at length throwing his galley, a wreck, on the shore, not far from the mouth of the Somme. The

Harold's Interview with Edward

galley itself was broken up, but Harold and his company escaped to land. They found that they were in the dominions of a certain prince who held possessions on that coast, whose style and title was Guy, count of Ponthieu.

The law in those days was, that wrecks became the property of the lord of the territory on the shores of which they occurred; and not only were the ships and the goods which they contained thus confiscated in case of such a disaster, but the owners themselves became liable to be seized and held captive for a ransom. Harold, knowing his danger, was attempting to secrete himself on the coast till he could get to Normandy, when a fisherman who saw him, and knew by his dress and appearance, and by the deference with which he was treated by the rest of the company, that he was a man of great consequence in his native land, went to the count, and said that for ten crowns he would show him where there was a man who would be worth a thousand to him. The count came down with his retinue to the coast, seized the unfortunate adventurers, took possession of all the goods and baggage that the waves had spared, and shut the men themselves up in his castle at Abbeville till they could pay their ransom.

Harold remonstrated against this treatment. He said that he was on his way to Normandy on business of great importance with the duke, from the King of England, and that he could not be detained. But the count was very decided in refusing to let him go without his ransom. Harold then sent word to William, acquainting him with his situation, and asking him to effect his release. William sent to the count, demanding that he should give his prisoner up. All these things, however, only tended to elevate and enlarge the count's ideas of the value and importance of the prize which he had been so fortunate to secure. He persisted in refusing to give him up without ransom. Finally William paid the ransom, in the shape of a large sum of money, and the cession, in addition, of a considerable territory. Harold and his companions in bondage were then delivered to William's messengers, and conducted by them in safety to Rouen, where William was then residing.

William received his distinguished guest with every possible mark of the most honorable consideration. He was escorted with great parade and ceremony into the palace, lodged in the most sumptuous manner, provided with every necessary supply, and games, and military spectacles, and feasts and entertainments without number, were arranged to celebrate his visit. William informed him that he was at liberty to return to England whenever he pleased, and that his brother and his nephew, the hostages that he had come to seek, were at his disposal. He, however, urged him not to return immediately, but to remain a short time in Normandy with his companions. Harold accepted the invitation.

All this exuberance of hospitality had its origin, as the reader will readily divine, in the duke's joy in finding the only important rival likely to appear to contest his claims to the English crown so fully in his power, and in the hope which he entertained of so managing affairs at this visit as to divert Harold's mind from the idea of becoming the King of England himself, and to induce him to pledge himself to act in his, that is, William's favor. He took, therefore, all possible pains to make him enjoy his visit in Normandy; he exhibited to him the wealth and the resources of the country—conducting him from place to place to visit the castles, the abbeys, and the towns—and, finally, he proposed that he should accompany him on a military expedition into Brittany.

Harold, pleased with the honors conferred upon him, and with the novelty and magnificence of the scenes to which he was introduced, entered heartily into all these plans, and his companions and attendants were no less pleased than he. William knighted many of these followers of Harold, and made them costly presents of horses, and banners, and suits of armor, and other such gifts as were calculated to captivate the hearts of martial adventurers such as they. William soon gained an entire ascendency over their minds, and when he invited them to accompany him on his expedition into Brittany, they were all eager to go.

Brittany was west of Normandy, and on the frontiers of it, so that the expedition was not a distant one. Nor was it long protracted. It was, in fact, a sort of pleasure excursion, William taking his guest across the frontier into his neighbor's territory, on a marauding party, just as a nobleman, in modern times, would take a party into a forest to hunt. William and Harold were on the most intimate and friendly terms possible during the continuance of this campaign. They occupied the same tent, and ate at the same table. Harold evinced great military talents and much bravery in the various adventures which they met with in Brittany, and William felt more than ever the desirableness of securing his influence on his, that is, William's side, or, at least, of preventing his becoming an open rival and enemy. On their return from Brittany into Normandy, he judged that the time had arrived for taking his measures. He accordingly resolved to come to an open understanding with Harold in respect to his plans, and to seek his co-operation.

He introduced the subject, the historians say, one day as they were riding along homeward from their excursion, and had been for some time talking familiarly on the way, relating tales to one another of wars, battles, sieges, and hair-breadth escapes, and other such adventures as formed, generally, the subjects of narrative conversation in those days. At length William, finding Harold, as he judged, in a favorable mood for such a communication, introduced the subject of the English realm and the approaching demise of the crown. He told him, confidentially, that there had been an arrangement between him, William, and King Edward, for some time, that Edward was to *adopt* him as his successor. William told Harold, moreover, that he should rely a great deal on his co-operation and assistance in getting peaceable possession of the kingdom, and promised to bestow upon him the very highest rewards and honors in return if he would give him his aid. The only rival claimant, William said, was the young child Edgar, and he had no friends, no party, no military forces, and no means whatever for maintaining his pretensions. On the other hand, he, William, and Harold, had obviously all the power in their own hands, and if they could only co-operate together on a common understanding, they would be sure to have the power and the honors of the English realm entirely at their disposal.

Harold listened to all these suggestions, and pretended to be interested and pleased. He was, in reality, interested, but he was not pleased. He wished to secure the kingdom for himself, not merely to obtain a share, however large, of its power and its honors as the subject of another. He was, however, too wary to evince his displeasure. On the contrary, he assented to the plan, professed to enter into it with all his heart, and expressed his readiness to commence, immediately, the necessary preliminary measures for carrying it into execution. William was much gratified with the successful result of his negotiation, and the two chieftains rode home to William's palace in Normandy, banded together, apparently, by very strong ties. In secret, however, Harold was resolving to effect his departure from Normandy as soon as possible, and to make immediate and most effectual measures for securing the kingdom of England to himself, without any regard to the promises that he had made to William.

Nor must it be supposed that William himself placed any positive reliance on mere promises from Harold. He immediately began to form plans for binding him to the performance of his stipulations, by the modes then commonly employed for securing the fulfillment of covenants made among princes. These methods were three—intermarriages, the giving of hostages, and solemn oaths.

William proposed two marriages as means of strengthening the alliance between himself and Harold. Harold was to give to William one of his daughters, that William might marry her to one of his Norman chieftains. This would be, of course, placing her in William's power, and making her a hostage all but in name. Harold, however, consented. The second marriage proposed was between William's daughter and Harold himself; but as his daughter was a child of only seven years of age, it could only be a betrothment that could take place at that time. Harold acceded to this proposal too, and arrangements were made for having the faith of the parties pledged to one another in the most solemn manner. A great assembly of all the knights, nobles, and ladies of the court was convened, and the ceremony of pledging the troth between the fierce warrior and the gentle and wondering child was performed with as much pomp and parade as if it had been an actual wedding. The name of the girl was Adela.

In respect to hostages, William determined to detain one of those whom Harold, as will be recollected, had come into Normandy to recover. He told him, therefore, that he might take with him his nephew Hacune, but that Ulnoth, his brother, should remain, and William would bring him over himself when he came to take possession of the kingdom. Harold was extremely unwilling to leave his brother thus in William's power; but as he knew very well that his being allowed to return to England himself would depend upon his not evincing any reluctance to giving William security, or manifesting any other indication that he was not intending to keep his plighted faith, he readily consented, and it was thus settled that Ulnoth should remain.

Finally, in order to hold Harold to the fulfillment of his promises by every possible form of obligation, William proposed that he should take a public and solemn oath, in the presence of a large assembly of all the great potentates and chieftains of the realm, by which he should bind himself, under the most awful sanctions, to keep his word. Harold made no objection to this either. He considered himself as, in fact, in duress, and his actions as not free. He was in William's power, and was influenced in all he did by a desire to escape from Normandy, and once more recover his liberty. He accordingly decided, in his own mind, that whatever oaths he might take he should afterward consider as forced upon him, and consequently as null and void, and was ready, therefore, to take any that William might propose.

The great assembly was accordingly convened. In the middle of the council hall there was placed a great chair of state, which was covered with a cloth of gold. Upon this cloth, and raised considerably above the seat, was the *missal*, that is, the book of service of the Catholic Church, written on parchment and splendidly illuminated. The book was open at a passage from one of the Evangelists—the Evangelists being a portion of the Holy Scriptures which was, in those days, supposed to invest an oath with the most solemn sanctions.

Harold felt some slight misgivings as he advanced in the midst of such an imposing scene as the great assembly of knights and ladies presented in the council hall, to repeat his promises in the very presence of God, and to imprecate the retributive curses of the Almighty on the violation of them, which he was deliberately and fully determined to incur. He had, however, gone too far to retreat now. He advanced, therefore, to the open missal, laid his hand upon the book, and, repeating the words which William dictated to him from his throne, he took the threefold oath required, namely, to aid William to the utmost of his power in his attempt to secure the succession to the English crown, to marry William's daughter Adela as soon as she should arrive at a suitable age, and to send over forthwith from England his own daughter, that she might be espoused to one of William's nobles.

As soon as the oath was thus taken, William caused the missal and the cloth of gold to be removed, and there appeared beneath it, on the chair of state, a chest, containing the sacred relics of the Church, which William had secretly collected from the abbeys and monasteries of his dominions, and placed in this concealment, that, without Harold's being conscious of it, their dreadful sanction might be added to that which the Holy Evangelists imposed. These relics were fragments of bones set in caskets and frames, and portions of blood—relics, as the monks alleged, of apostles or of the Savior—and small pieces of wood, similarly preserved, which had been portions of the cross of Christ or of his thorny crown. These things were treasured up with great solemnity in the monastic establishments and in the churches of these early times, and were regarded with a veneration and awe, of which it is almost beyond our power even to conceive. Harold trembled when he saw what he had unwittingly done. He was terrified to think how much more dreadful was the force of the imprecations that he had uttered than he had imagined while uttering them. But it was too late to undo what he had done. The assembly was finally dismissed. William thought he had the conscience of his new ally firmly secured, and Harold began to prepare for leaving Normandy.

He continued on excellent terms with William until his departure. William accompanied him to the sea-shore when the time of his embarkation arrived, and dismissed him at last with many farewell honors, and a profusion of presents. Harold set sail, and, crossing the Channel in safety, he landed in England.

He commenced immediately an energetic system of measures to strengthen his own cause, and prepare the way for his own accession. He organized his party, collected arms and munitions of war, and did all that he could to ingratiate himself with the most powerful and wealthy nobles. He sought the favor of the king, too, and endeavored to persuade him to discard William. The king was now old and infirm, and was growing more and more inert and gloomy as he advanced in age. His mind was occupied altogether in ecclesiastical rites and observances, or plunged in a torpid and lifeless melancholy, which made him averse to giving any thought to the course which the affairs of his kingdom were to take after he was gone. He did not care whether Harold or William took the crown when he laid it aside, provided they would allow him to die in peace.

He had had, a few years previous to this time, a plan of making a pilgrimage to Jerusalem, but had finally made an arrangement with the pope, allowing him to build a Cathedral church, to be dedicated to St. Peter, a few miles west of London, in lieu of his pilgrimage. There was already a Cathedral church or *minster* in the heart of London which was dedicated to St. Paul. The new one was afterward often called, to distinguish it from the other, the *west* minster, which designation, Westminster, became afterward its regular name. It was on this spot, where Westminster Abbey now stands, that Edward's church was to be built. It was just completed at the time of which we are speaking, and the king was preparing for the dedication of it. He summoned an assembly of all the prelates and great ecclesiastical dignitaries of the land to convene at London, in order to dedicate the new Cathedral. Before they were ready for the service, the king was taken suddenly sick. They placed him upon his couch in his palace chamber, where he lay, restless, and moaning in pain, and repeating incessantly, half in sleep and half in delirium, the gloomy and threatening texts of Scripture which seemed to haunt his mind. He was eager to have the dedication go on, and they hastened the service in order to gratify him by having it performed before he died. The next day he was obviously failing. Harold and his friends were very earnest to have the departing monarch declare in *his* favor before he died, and their coming and going, and their loud discussions, rude soldiers as they were, disturbed his dying hours. He sent them word to choose whom they would for king, duke or earl, it was indifferent to him, and thus expired.

Harold had made his arrangements so well, and had managed so effectually to secure the influence of all the powerful nobles of the kingdom, that they immediately convened and offered him the crown. Edgar was in the court of Edward at the time, but he was too young to make any effort to advance his claims. He was, in fact, a foreigner, though in the English royal line. He had been brought up on the Continent of Europe, and could not even speak the English tongue. He acquiesced, therefore, without complaint, in these proceedings, and was even present as a consenting spectator on the occasion of Harold's coronation, which ceremony was performed with great pomp and parade, at St. Paul's, in London, very soon after King Edward's death. Harold rewarded Edgar for his complaisance and discretion by conferring upon him the honor of knighthood immediately after the coronation, and in the church where the ceremony was performed. He also conferred similar distinctions and honors upon many other aspiring and ambitious men whom he wished to secure to his side. He thus seemed to have secure and settled possession of the throne.

Previously to this time, Harold had married a young lady of England, a sister of two very powerful noblemen, and the richest heiress in the realm. This marriage greatly strengthened his influence in England, and helped to prepare the way for his accession to the supreme power.

The tidings of it, however, when they crossed the Channel and reached the ears of William of Normandy, as the act was an open and deliberate violation of one of the covenants which Harold had made with William, convinced the latter that none of these covenants would be kept, and prepared him to expect all that afterward followed.

8

The Preparations

A.D. 1066

Harold's brother Tostig.—He brings intelligence of Harold's accession. —William's strength and dexterity.—His surprise.—Fitzosborne.—His interview with William.—The great council of state.—The embassy to Harold.—Harold reminded of his promises.—His replies.—Return of the messenger.—William prepares for war.—William calls a general council.—Want of funds.—Means of raising money.—Adverse views.— Various opinions.—Confusion and disorder.—Plan of Fitzosborne.—It is adopted by William.—Success of Fitzosborne's plan.—Supplies flow in liberally.—Embassage to the pope.—Its success.—Reasons why the pope favored William's claims.—The banner and the ring.—Excitement produced by their reception.—William's proclamations.—Their effects. —William's promises.—Naval preparations.—Philip, king of France. —William's visit to him.—William's interview with Philip.—Philip opposes his plans.—Council of nobles.—Result of their deliberations.— William's return.—Final preparations.—Matilda made duchess regent. —William's motives.—Republican sentiments.—Hereditary sovereigns. —Enthusiasm of the people.—The two-tailed comet.

THE messenger who brought William the tidings of Harold's accession to the throne was a man named Tostig, Harold's brother. Though he was Harold's brother, he was still his bitterest enemy. Brothers are seldom friends in families where there is a crown to be contended for. There were, of course, no public modes of communicating intelligence in those days, and Tostig had learned the facts of Edward's death and Harold's coronation through spies which he had stationed at certain points on the coast. He was himself, at that time, on the Continent. He rode with all speed to Rouen to communicate the news to William, eager to incite him to commence hostilities against his brother.

William Receiving Tostig's Tidings

When Tostig arrived at Rouen, William was in a park which lay in the vicinity of the city, trying a new bow that had been recently made for him. William was a man of prodigious muscular strength, and they gave him the credit of being able to use easily a bow which nobody else could bend. A part of this credit was doubtless due to the etiquette which, in royal palaces and grounds, leads all sensible courtiers to take good care never to succeed in attempts to excel the king. But, notwithstanding this consideration, there is no doubt that the duke really merited a great portion of the commendation that he received for his strength and dexterity in the use of the bow. It was a weapon in which he took great interest. A new one had been made for him, of great elasticity and strength, and he had gone out into his park, with his officers, to try its powers, when Tostig arrived. Tostig followed him to the place, and there advancing to his side, communicated the tidings to him privately.

William was greatly moved by the intelligence. His arrow dropped upon the ground. He gave the bow to an attendant. He stood for a time speechless, tying and untying the cordon of his cloak in his abstraction. Presently he began slowly to move away from the place, and to return toward the city. His attendants followed him in silence, wondering what the exciting tidings could be which had produced so sudden and powerful an effect.

William went into the castle hall, and walked to and fro a long time, thoughtful, and evidently agitated. His attendants waited in silence, afraid to speak to him. Rumors began at length to circulate among them in respect to the nature of the intelligence which had been received. At length a great officer of state, named Fitzosborne, arrived at the castle. As he passed through the courtyard and gates, the attendants and the people, knowing that he possessed in a great degree the confidence of his sovereign, asked him what the tidings were that had made such an impression. "I know nothing certain about it," said he, "but I will soon learn." So saying, he advanced toward William, and accosted him by saying, "Why should you conceal from us your news? It is reported in the city that the King of England is dead, and that Harold has violated his oaths to you, and has seized the kingdom. Is that true?"

William acknowledged that that was the intelligence by which he had been so vexed and chagrined. Fitzosborne urged the duke not to allow such events to depress or dispirit him. "As for the death of Edward," said he, "that is an event past and sure, and cannot be recalled; but Harold's usurpation and treachery admits of a very easy remedy. You have the right to the throne, and you have the soldiers necessary to enforce that right. Undertake the enterprise boldly. You will be sure to succeed."

William revolved the subject in his mind for a few days, during which the exasperation and anger which the first receipt of the intelligence had produced upon him was succeeded by calm but indignant deliberation, in respect to the course which he should pursue. He concluded to call a great council of state, and to lay the case before them—not for the purpose of obtaining their advice, but to call their attention to the crisis in a formal and solemn manner, and to prepare them to act in concert in the subsequent measures to be pursued. The result of the deliberations of this council, guided, doubtless, by William's own designs, was, that the first step should be to send an embassy to Harold to demand of him the fulfillment of his promises.

The messenger was accordingly dispatched. He proceeded to London and laid before Harold the communication with which he had been entrusted. This communication recounted the three promises which Harold had made, namely, to send his daughter to Normandy to be married to one of William's generals; to marry William's daughter himself; and to maintain William's claims to the English crown on the death of Edward. He was to remind Harold, also, of the solemnity with which he had bound himself to fulfill these obligations, by oaths taken in the presence of the most sacred relics of the Church, and in the most public and deliberate manner.

Harold replied,

1. That as to sending over his daughter to be married to one of William's generals, he could not do it, for his daughter was dead. He presumed, he said, that William did not wish him to send the corpse.

2. In respect to marrying William's daughter, to whom he had been affianced in Normandy, he was sorry to say that that was also out of his power, as he could not take a foreign wife without the consent of his people, which he was confident would never be given; besides, he was already married, he said, to a Saxon lady of his own dominions.

3. In regard to the kingdom: it did not depend upon him, he said, to decide who should rule over England as Edward's successor, but

upon the will of Edward himself, and upon the English people. The English barons and nobles had decided, with Edward's concurrence, that he, Harold, was their legitimate and proper sovereign, and that it was not for him to controvert their will. However much he might be disposed to comply with William's wishes, and to keep his promise, it was plain that it was out of his power, for in promising him the English crown, he had promised what did not belong to him to give.

4. As to his oaths, he said that, notwithstanding the secret presence of the sacred relics under the cloth of gold, he considered them as of no binding force upon his conscience, for he was constrained to take them as the only means of escaping from the duress in which he was virtually held in Normandy. Promises, and oaths even, when extorted by necessity, were null and void.

The messenger returned to Normandy with these replies, and William immediately began to prepare for war.

His first measure was to call a council of his most confidential friends and advisers, and to lay the subject before them. They cordially approved of the plan of an invasion of England, and promised to cooperate in the accomplishment of it to the utmost of their power.

The next step was to call a general council of all the chieftains and nobles of the land, and also the *notables*, as they were called, or principal officers and municipal authorities of the *towns*. The main point of interest for the consideration of this assembly was, whether the country would submit to the necessary taxation for raising the necessary funds. William had ample power, as duke, to decide upon the invasion and to undertake it. He could also, without much difficulty, raise the necessary number of men; for every baron in his realm was bound, by the feudal conditions on which he held his land, to furnish his quota of men for any military enterprise in which his sovereign might see fit to engage. But for so distant and vast an undertaking as this, William needed a much larger supply of *funds* than were usually required in the wars of those days. For raising such large supplies, the political institutions of the Middle Ages had not made any adequate provision. Governments then had no power of taxation, like that so freely exercised in modern times; and even now, taxes in France and England take the form of *grants* from the people to the kings. And as to the contrivance, so exceedingly ingenious, by which inexhaustible resources are opened to governments at the present day—that is, the plan of borrowing the money, and leaving posterity to pay or repudiate the debt, as they please, no minister of finance had, in William's day, been brilliant enough to discover it. Thus each ruler had to rely, then, mainly on the rents and income from his own lands, and other private resources, for the comparatively small amount of money that he needed in his brief campaigns. But now William perceived that ships must be built and equipped, and great stores of provisions accumulated, and arms and munitions of war provided, all which would require a considerable outlay; and how was this money to be obtained?

The general assembly which he convened were greatly distracted by the discussion of the question. The quiet and peaceful citizens who inhabited the towns, the artisans and tradesmen, who wished for nothing but to be allowed to go on in their industrial pursuits in peace, were opposed to the whole project. They thought it unreasonable and absurd that they should be required to contribute from their earnings to enable their lord and master to go off on so distant and desperate an undertaking, from which, even if successful, they could derive no benefit whatever. Many of the barons, too, were opposed to the scheme. They thought it very likely to end in disaster and defeat; and they denied that their feudal obligation to furnish men for their sovereign's wars was binding to the extent of requiring them to go out of the country, and beyond the sea, to prosecute his claims to the throne of another kingdom.

Others, on the other hand, among the members of William's assembly, were strongly disposed to favor the plan. They were more ardent or more courageous than the rest, or perhaps their position and circumstances were such that they had more to hope from the success of the enterprise than they, or less to fear from its failure. Thus there was great diversity of opinion; and as the parliamentary system of rules, by which a body of turbulent men, in modern times, are kept in some semblance of organization and order during a debate, had not then been developed, the meeting of these Norman deliberators was, for a time, a scene of uproar and confusion. The members gathered in groups, each speaker getting around him as many as he could obtain to listen to his harangue; the more quiet and passive portion of the assembly moving to and fro, from group to group, as they were attracted by the earnestness and eloquence of the different speakers, or by their approval of the sentiments which they heard them expressing. The scene, in fact, was like that presented in exciting times by a political caucus in America, before it is called to order by the chairman.

Fitzosborne, the confidential friend and counselor, who has already been mentioned as the one who ventured to accost the duke at the time when the tidings of Edward's death and of Harold's accession first reached him, now seeing that anything like definite and harmonious action on the part of this tumultuous assembly was out of the question, went to the duke, and proposed to him to give up the assembly as such, and make the best terms and arrangements that he could with the constituent elements of it, individually and severally. He would himself, he said, furnish forty ships, manned, equipped, and provisioned; and he recommended to the duke to call each of the others into his presence, and ask them what they were individually willing to do. The duke adopted this plan, and it was wonderfully successful. Those who were first invited made large offers, and their offers were immediately registered in form by the proper officers. Each one who followed was emulous of the example of those who had preceded him, and desirous of evincing as much zeal and generosity as they. Then, besides, the duke received these vassals with so much condescension and urbanity, and treated them with so much consideration and respect, as greatly to flatter their vanity, and raise them in their own estimation, by exalting their ideas of the importance of the services which they could render in carrying so vast an enterprise to a successful result. In a word, the tide turned like a flood in favor of granting liberal supplies. The nobles and knights promised freely men, money, ships, arms, provisions—everything, in short, that was required; and when the work of receiving and registering the offers was completed, and the officers summed up the aggregate amount, William found, to his extreme satisfaction, that his wants were abundantly supplied.

There was another very important point, which William adopted immediate measures to secure, and that was obtaining the *Pope's* approval of his intended expedition. The moral influence of having the Roman pontiff on his side, would, he knew, be of incalculable advantage to him. He sent an embassage, accordingly, to Rome, to lay the whole subject before his holiness, and to pray that the pope would declare that he was justly entitled to the English crown, and authorize him to proceed and take possession of it by force of arms. Lanfranc was the messenger whom he employed—the same Lanfranc who had been so successful, some years before, in the negotiations at Rome connected with the confirmation of William and Matilda's marriage.

Lanfranc was equally successful now. The pope, after examining William's claims, pronounced them valid. He decided that William was entitled to the rank and honors of King of England. He caused a formal diploma to be made out to this effect. The diploma was elegantly executed, signed with the cross, according to the pontifical custom, and sealed with a round leaden seal. [The Latin name for such a seal was *bulla*. It is on account of this sort of seal, which is customarily affixed to them, that papal edicts have received the name of *bulls*.]

It was, in fact, very natural that the Roman authorities should take a favorable view of William's enterprise, and feel an interest in its success, as it was undoubtedly for the interest of the Church that William, rather than Harold, should reign over England, as the accession of William would bring the English realm far more fully under the influence of the Roman Church. William had always been very submissive to the pontifical authority, as was shown in his conduct in respect to the question of his marriage. He himself, and also Matilda his wife, had always taken a warm interest in the welfare and prosperity of the abbeys, the monasteries, the churches, and the other religious establishments of the times. Then the very circumstance that he sent his ambassador to Rome to submit his claims to the pontiff's adjudication, while Harold did not do so, indicated a greater deference for the authority of the Church, and made it probable that he would be a far more obedient and submissive son of the Church, in his manner of ruling his realm, if he should succeed in gaining possession of it, than Harold his rival. The pope and his counselors at Rome thought it proper to take all these things into the account in deciding between William and Harold, as they honestly believed, without doubt, that it was their first and highest duty to exalt and aggrandize, by every possible means, the spiritual authority of the sacred institution over which they were called to preside.

The pope and his cardinals, accordingly, espoused William's cause very warmly. In addition to the diploma which gave William formal authority to take possession of the English crown, the pope sent him a banner and a ring. The banner was of costly and elegant workmanship; its value, however, did not consist in its elegance or its cost, but in a solemn benediction which his holiness pronounced over it, by which it was rendered sacred and inviolable. The banner, thus blessed, was forwarded to William by Lanfranc with great care.

It was accompanied by the ring. The ring was of gold, and it contained a diamond of great value. The gold and the diamond both, however, served only as settings to preserve and honor something of far greater value than they. This choice treasure was a hair from the head of the Apostle Peter! a sacred relic of miraculous virtue and of inestimable value.

When the edict with its leaden seal, and the banner and the ring arrived in Normandy, they produced a great and universal excitement. To have bestowed upon the enterprise thus emphatically the solemn sanction of the great spiritual head of the Church, to whom the great mass of the people looked up with an awe and a reverence almost divine, was to seal indissolubly the rightfulness of the enterprise, and to ensure its success. There was thenceforward no difficulty in procuring men or means. Everybody was eager to share in the glory, and to obtain the rewards, of an enterprise thus commended by an authority duly commissioned to express, in all such cases, the judgment of Heaven.

Finding that the current was thus fairly setting in his favor, William sent proclamations into all the countries surrounding Normandy, inviting knights, and soldiers, and adventurers of every degree to join him in his projected enterprise. These proclamations awakened universal attention. Great numbers of adventurous men determined to enter William's service. Horses, arms, and accoutrements were everywhere in great demand. The invasion of England and the question of joining it were the universal topics of conversation. The roads were covered with knights and soldiers, some on horseback and alone, others in bands, large or small, all proceeding to Normandy to tender their services. William received them all, and made liberal promises to bestow rewards and honors upon them in England, in the event of his success. To some he offered pay in money; to others, booty; to others, office and power. Everyone had his price. Even the priests and dignitaries of the Church shared the general enthusiasm. One of them furnished a ship and twenty armed men, under an agreement to be appointed bishop of a certain valuable English diocese when William should be established on his throne.

While all these movements were going on in the interior of the country, all the seaports and towns along the coast of Normandy presented a very busy scene of naval preparation. Naval architects were employed in great numbers in building and fitting out vessels. Some were constructed and furnished for the transportation of men, others for conveying provisions and munitions of war; and lighters and boats were built for ascending the rivers, and for aiding in landing troops upon shelving shores. Smiths and armorers were occupied incessantly in manufacturing spears, and swords, and coats of mail; while vast numbers of laboring men and beasts of burden were employed in conveying arms and materials to and from the manufactories to the ships, and from one point of embarkation to another.

As soon as William had put all these busy agencies thus in successful operation, he considered that there was one more point which it was necessary for him to secure before finally embarking, and that was the co-operation and aid of the French king, whose name at this time was Philip. In his character of Duke of Normandy the King of France was his liege lord, and he was bound to act, in some degree, under an acknowledgment of his superior authority. In his new capacity, that is, as King of England, or, rather, as heir to the English kingdom, he was, of course, wholly independent of Philip, and, consequently, not bound by any feudal obligation to look to him at all. He thought it most prudent, however, to attempt, at least, to conciliate Philip's favor, and, accordingly, leaving his officers and his workmen to go on with the work of organizing his army and of building and equipping the fleet, he set off, himself, on an expedition to the court of the French king. He thought it safer to undertake this delicate mission himself, rather than to intrust it to an ambassador or deputy.

He found Philip at his palace of St. Germain's, which was situated at a short distance from Paris. The duke assumed, in his interview with the king, a very respectful and deferential air and manner. Philip was a very young man, though haughty and vain. William was very much his superior, not only in age and experience, but in talents and character, and in personal renown. Still, he approached the monarch with all the respectful observance due from a vassal to his sovereign, made known his plans, and asked for Philip's approbation and aid. He was willing, he said, in case that aid was afforded him, to hold his kingdom of England, as he had done the duchy of Normandy, as a dependency of the French crown.

Philip seemed not at all disposed to look upon the project with favor. He asked William who was going to take care of his duchy while he was running off after a kingdom. William replied, at first, that that was a subject which he did not think his neighbors need concern themselves about. Then thinking, on reflection, that a more respectful answer would be more politic, under the circumstances of the case, he added, that he was providentially blessed with a prudent wife and loving subjects, and that he thought he might safely leave his domestic affairs in their hands until he should return. Philip still opposed the plan. It was Quixotic, he said, and dangerous. He strongly advised William to abandon the scheme, and be content with his present possessions. Such desperate schemes of ambition as those he was contemplating would only involve him in ruin.

Before absolutely deciding the case, however, Philip called a council of his great nobles and officers of state, and laid William's proposals before them. The result of their deliberations was to confirm Philip in his first decision. They said that the rendering to William the aid which he desired would involve great expense, and be attended with great danger; and as to William's promises to hold England as a vassal of the King of France, they had no faith in the performance of them. It had been very difficult, they said, for many years, for the kings of France to maintain any effectual authority over the dukes of Normandy, and when once master of so distant and powerful a realm as England, all control over them would be sundered forever.

Philip then gave William his final answer in accordance with these counsels. The answer was received, on William's part, with strong feelings of disappointment and displeasure. Philip conducted the duke to his retinue when the hour of departure arrived, in order to soothe, as far as possible, his irritated feelings, by dismissing him from his court with marks of his honorable consideration and regard. William, however, was not in a mood to be pleased. He told Philip, on taking leave of him, that he was losing the most powerful vassal that any lord sovereign ever had, by the course which he had decided to pursue. "I would have held the whole realm of England as a part of your dominions, acknowledging you as sovereign over all, if you had consented to render me your aid, but I will not do it since you refuse. I shall feel bound to repay only those who assist me."

William returned to Normandy, where all the preparations for the expedition had been going on with great vigor during his absence, and proceeded to make arrangements for the last great measure which it was necessary to take previous to his departure; that was, the regular constitution of a government to rule in Normandy while he should be gone. He determined to leave the supreme power in the hands of his wife Matilda, appointing, at the same time, a number of civil and military officers as a council of regency, who were to assist her in her deliberations by giving her information and advice, and to manage, under her direction, the different departments of the government. Her title was "Duchess Regent," and she was installed into her office in a public and solemn manner, at a great assembly of the estates of the realm. At the close of the ceremonies, after William had given Matilda his charge, he closed his address by adding, "And do not let us fail to enjoy the benefit of your prayers, and those of all the ladies of your court, that the blessing of God may attend us, and secure the success of our expedition."

We are not necessarily to suppose, as we might at first be strongly inclined to do, that there was any special hypocrisy and pretense in William's thus professing to rely on the protection of Heaven in the personal and political dangers which he was about to incur. It is probable that he honestly believed that the inheritance of the English crown was his right, and, that being the case, that a vigorous and manly effort to enforce his right was a solemn duty. In the present age of the world, now that there are so many countries in which intelligence, industry, and love of order are so extensively diffused that the mass of the community are capable of organizing and administering a government themselves, republicans are apt to look upon hereditary sovereigns as despots, ruling only for the purpose of promoting their own aggrandizement, and the ends of an unholy and selfish ambition. That there have been a great many such despots no one can deny; but then, on the other hand, there have been many others who have acted, in a greater or less degree, under the influence of principles of duty in their political career. They have honestly believed that the vast power with which, in coming forward into life, they have found themselves invested, without, in most cases, any agency of their own, was a trust imposed upon them by divine Providence, which could not innocently be laid aside; that on them devolved the protection of the communities over which they ruled from external hostility, and the preservation of peace and order within, and the promotion of the general industry and welfare, as an imperious and solemn duty; and they have devoted their lives to the performance of this duty, with the usual mixture, it is true, of ambition and selfishness, but still, after all, with as much conscientiousness and honesty as the mass of men in the humbler walks of life evince in performing theirs. William of Normandy appears to have been one of this latter class; and in obeying the dictates of his ambition in seeking to gain possession of the English crown, he no doubt considered himself as fulfilling the obligations of duty too.

However this may be, he went on with his preparations in the most vigorous and prosperous manner. The whole country were enthusiastic in the cause; and their belief that the enterprise about to be undertaken had unquestionably secured the favor of Heaven, was confirmed by an extraordinary phenomenon which occurred just before the armament was ready to set sail. A comet appeared in the sky, which, as close observers declared, had a double tail. It was universally agreed that this portended that England and Normandy were about to be combined, and to form a double kingdom, which should exhibit to all mankind a wonderful spectacle of splendor.

9

Crossing the Channel

A.D. 1066

The River Dive.—Final assembling of the fleet.—Map.—Brilliant and magnificent scene.—Equinoctial gales.—The expedition detained by them.—Injurious effects of the storm.—Discouragement of the men.—Fears and forebodings.—Some of the vessels wrecked.—Favorable change. —The fleet puts to sea.—Various delays.—Its effects.—Harold's want of information.—He withdraws his troops.—Harold's vigilance.—He sends spies into Normandy.—Harold's spies.—They are detected.—William dismisses the spies.—His confidence in his cause.—Fears of William's officers.—He reassures them.—Arrival of Matilda with the Mira.—A present to William.—The squadron puts to sea again.—Its appearance.—Fleetness of the Mira.—Leaves the fleet out of sight.—William's unconcern.—Reappearance of the fleet.—The fleet enters the Bay of Pevensey. —Disembarkation.—Landing of the troops.—Anecdote.—The encampment.—Scouts sent out.—William's supper.—The missing ships.—The Conqueror's Stone.—March of the army.—Flight of the inhabitants.—The army encamps.—The town of Hastings.—William's fortifications.—Approach of Harold.

THE place for the final assembling of the fleet which was to convey the expedition across the Channel was the mouth of a small river called the Dive, which will be seen upon the following map, flowing from the neighborhood of the castle of Falaise northward into the sea. The grand gathering took place in the beginning of the month of September, in the year 1066. This date, which marks the era of the Norman Conquest, is one of the dates which students of history fix indelibly in the memory.

Map of Normandy

The gathering of the fleet in the estuary of the Dive, and the assembling of the troops on the beach along its shores, formed a very grand and imposing spectacle. The fleets of galleys, ships, boats, and barges covering the surface of the water—the long lines of tents under the cliffs on the land—the horsemen, splendidly mounted, and glittering with steel—the groups of soldiers, all busily engaged in transporting provisions and stores to and fro, or making the preliminary arrangements for the embarkation—the thousands of spectators who came and went incessantly, and the duke himself, gorgeously dressed, and mounted on his war-horse, with the guards and officers that attended him—these, and the various other elements of martial parade and display usually witnessed on such occasions, conspired to produce a very gay and brilliant, as well as magnificent scene.

Of course, the assembling of so large a force of men and of vessels, and the various preparations for the embarkation, consumed some time, and when at length all was ready—which was early in September—the equinoctial gales came on, and it was found impossible to leave the port. There was, in fact, a continuance of heavy winds and seas, and stormy skies, for several weeks. Short intervals, from time to time, occurred, when the clouds would break away, and the sun appear; but these intervals did not liberate the fleet from its confinement, for they were not long enough in duration to allow the sea to go down. The surf continued to come rolling and thundering in upon the shore, and over the sand-bars at the mouth of the river, making destruction the almost inevitable destiny of any ship which should undertake to brave its fury. The state of the skies gradually robbed the scene of the gay and brilliant colors which first it wore. The vessels furled their sails, and drew in their banners, and rode at anchor, presenting their heads doggedly to the storm. The men on the shore sought shelter in their tents. The spectators retired to their homes, while the duke and his officers watched the scudding clouds in the sky, day after day, with great and increasing anxiety.

In fact, William had very serious cause for apprehension in respect to the effect which this long-continued storm was to have on the success of his enterprise. The delay was a very serious consideration in itself, for the winter would soon be drawing near. In one month more it would seem to be out of the question for such a vast armament to cross the Channel at all. Then, when men are embarking in such dark and hazardous undertakings as that in which William was now engaged, their spirits and their energy rise and sink in great fluctuations, under the influence of very slight and inadequate causes; and nothing has greater influence over them at such times than the aspect of the skies. William found that the ardor and enthusiasm of his army were fast disappearing under the effects of chilling winds and driving rain. The feelings of discontent and depression which the frowning expression of the heavens awakened in their minds, were deepened and spread by the influence of sympathy. The men had nothing to do, during the long and dreary hours of the day, but to anticipate hardships and dangers, and to entertain one another, as they watched the clouds driving along the cliffs, and the rolling of the surges in the offing, with anticipations of shipwrecks, battles, and defeats, and all the other gloomy forebodings which haunt the imagination of a discouraged and discontented soldier.

Nor were these ideas of wrecks and destruction wholly imaginary. Although the body of the fleet remained in the river, where it was sheltered from the winds, yet there were many cases of single ships that were from time to time exposed to them. These were detached vessels coming in late to the rendezvous, or small squadrons sent out to some neighboring port under some necessity connected with the preparations, or strong galleys, whose commanders, more bold than the rest, were willing, in cases *not* of absolute necessity, to brave the danger. Many of these vessels were wrecked. The fragments of them, with the bodies of the drowned mariners, were driven to the shore. The ghastly spectacles presented by these dead bodies, swollen and mangled, and half buried in the sand, as if the sea had been endeavoring to hide the mischief it had done, shocked and terrified the spectators who saw them. William gave orders to have all these bodies gathered up and interred secretly, as fast as they were found; still, exaggerated rumors of the number and magnitude of these disasters were circulated in the camp, and the discontent and apprehensions grew every day more and more alarming.

William resolved that he must put to sea at the very first possible opportunity. The favorable occasion was not long wanting. The wind changed. The storm appeared to cease. A breeze sprang up from the south, which headed back the surges from the French shore. William gave orders to embark. The tents were struck. The baggage of the soldiers was sent on board the transport vessels. The men themselves, crowded into great flat-bottomed boats, passed in masses to the ships from the shore. The spectators reappeared, and covered the cliffs and promontories near, to witness the final scene. The sails were hoisted, and the vast armament moved out upon the sea.

The appearance of a favorable change in the weather proved fallacious after all, for the clouds and storm returned, and after being driven, in apprehension and danger, about a hundred miles to the northeast along the coast, the fleet was compelled to seek refuge again in a harbor. The port which received them was St. Valery, near Dieppe. The duke was greatly disappointed at being obliged thus again to take the land. Still, the attempt to advance had not been a labor wholly lost; for as the French coast here trends to the northward, they had been gradually narrowing the channel as they proceeded, and were, in fact, so far on the way toward the English shores. Then there were, besides, some reasons for touching here, before the final departure, to receive some last reenforcements and supplies. William had also one more opportunity of communicating with his capital and with Matilda.

These delays, disastrous as they seemed to be, and ominous of evil, were nevertheless attended with one good effect, of which, however, William at the time was not aware. They led Harold, in England, to imagine that the enterprise was abandoned, and so put him off his guard. There were in those days, as has already been remarked, no regular and public modes of intercommunication, by which intelligence of important movements and events was spread every where, as now, with promptness and certainty. Governments were obliged, accordingly, to rely for information, in respect to what their enemies were doing, on rumors, or on the reports of spies. Rumors had gone to England in August that William was meditating an invasion, and Harold had made some extensive preparations to meet and oppose him; but, finding that he did not come—that week after week of September passed away, and no signs of an enemy appeared, and gaining no certain information of the causes of the delay, he concluded that the enterprise was abandoned, or else, perhaps, postponed to the ensuing spring. Accordingly, as the winter was coming on, he deemed it best to commence his preparations for sending his troops to their winter quarters. He disbanded some of them, and sent others away, distributing them in various castles and fortified towns, where they would be sheltered from the rigors of the season, and saved from the exposure and hardships of the camp, and yet, at the same time, remain within reach of a summons in case of any sudden emergency which might call for them. They were soon summoned, though not, in the first instance, to meet Harold, as will presently appear.

While adopting these measures, however, which he thought the comfort and safety of his army required, Harold did not relax his vigilance in watching, as well as he could, the designs and movements of his enemy. He kept his secret agents on the southern coast, ordering them to observe closely every thing that transpired, and to gather and send to him every item of intelligence which should find its way by any means across the Channel. Of course, William would do all in his power to intercept and cut off all communication, and he was, at this time, very much aided in these efforts by the prevalence of the storms, which made it almost impossible for the fishing and trading vessels of the coast to venture out to sea, or attempt to cross the Channel. The agents of Harold, therefore, on the southern coast of England, found that they could obtain but very little information.

At length the king, unwilling to remain any longer so entirely in the dark, resolved on sending some messengers across the sea into Normandy itself, to learn positively what the true state of the case might be. Messengers going thus secretly into the enemy's territory, or into the enemy's camp, become, by so doing, in martial law, *spies*, and incur, if they are taken, the penalty of death. The undertaking, therefore, is extremely hazardous; and as the death which is inflicted in cases of detection is an ignominious one—spies being hung, not shot—most men are very averse to encountering the danger. Still, desperate characters are always to be found in camps and armies, who are ready to undertake it on being promised very extraordinary pay.

Harold's spies contrived to make their way across the Channel, probably at some point far to the east of Normandy, where the passage is narrow. They then came along the shore, disguised as peasants of the country, and they arrived at St. Valery while William's fleets were there. Here they began to make their observations, scrutinizing every thing with close attention and care, and yet studiously endeavoring to conceal their interest in what they saw. Notwithstanding all their vigilance, however, they were discovered, proved to be spies, and taken before William to receive their sentence.

Instead of condemning them to death, which they undoubtedly supposed would be their inevitable fate, William ordered them to be set at liberty. "Go back," said he, "to King Harold, and tell him he might have saved himself the expense of sending spies into Normandy to learn what I am preparing for him. He will soon know by other means—much sooner, in fact, than he imagines. Go and tell him from me that he may put himself, if he pleases, in the safest place he can find in all his dominions, and if he does not find my hand upon him before the year is out, he never need fear me again as long as he lives."

Nor was this expression of confidence in the success of the measures which he was taking a mere empty boast. William knew the power of Harold, and he knew his own. The enterprise in which he had embarked was not a rash adventure. It was a cool, deliberate, well-considered plan. It appeared doubtful and dangerous in the eyes of mankind, for to mere superficial observers it seemed simply an aggressive war waged by a duke of Normandy, the ruler of a comparatively small and insignificant province, against a king of England, the monarch of one of the greatest and most powerful realms in the world. William, on the other hand, regarded it as an effort on the part of the rightful heir to a throne to dispossess a usurper. He felt confident of having the sympathy and co-operation of a great part of the community, even in England, the moment he could show them that he was able to maintain his rights; and that he could show them that, by a very decisive demonstration, was evident, visibly, before him, in the vast fleet which was riding at anchor in the harbor, and in the long lines of tents, filled with soldiery, which covered the land.

On one occasion, when some of his officers were expressing apprehensions of Harold's power, and their fears in respect to their being able successfully to cope with it, William replied, that the more formidable Harold's power should prove to be, the better he should be pleased, as the glory would be all the greater for them in having overcome it. "I have no objection," said he, "that you should entertain exalted ideas of his strength, though I wonder a little that you do not better appreciate our own. I need be under no concern lest he, at such a distance, should learn too much, by his spies, about the force which I am bringing against him, when you, who are so near me, seem to know so little about it. But do not give yourselves any concern. Trust to the justice of your cause and to my foresight. Perform your parts like men, and you will find that the result which I feel sure of, and you hope for, will certainly be attained."

The storm at length entirely cleared away, and the army and the fleet commenced their preparations for the final departure. In the midst of this closing scene, the attention of all the vast crowds assembled on board the ships and on the shores was one morning attracted by a beautiful ship which came sailing into the harbor. It proved to be a large and splendid vessel which the Duchess Matilda had built, at her own expense, and was now bringing in, to offer to her husband as her parting gift. She was herself on board, with her officers and attendants, having come to witness her husband's departure, and to bid him farewell. Her arrival, of course, under such circumstances, produced universal excitement and enthusiasm. The ships in harbor and the shores resounded with acclamations as the new arrival came gallantly in.

Matilda's vessel was finely built and splendidly decorated. The sails were of different colors, which gave it a very gay appearance. Upon them were painted, in various places, the three lions, which was the device of the Norman ensign. At the bows of the ship was an effigy, or figure-head, representing William and Matilda's second son shooting with a bow. This was the accomplishment which, of all others, his father took most interest in seeing his little son acquire. The arrow was drawn nearly to its head, indicating great strength in the little arms which were guiding it, and it was just ready to fly. The name of this vessel was the Mira. William made it his flag ship. He hoisted upon its mast head the consecrated banner which had been sent to him from Rome, and went on board accompanied by his officers and guards, and with great ceremony and parade.

At length the squadron was ready to put to sea. At a given signal the sails were hoisted, and the whole fleet began to move slowly out of the harbor. There were four hundred ships of large size, if we may believe the chronicles of the times, and more than a thousand transports. The decks of all these vessels were covered with men; banners were streaming from every mast and spar; and every salient point of the shore was crowded with spectators. The sea was calm, the air serene, and the mighty cloud of canvas which whitened the surface of the water moved slowly on over the gentle swell of the waves, forming a spectacle which, as a picture merely for the eye, was magnificent and grand, and, when regarded in connection with the vast results to the human race which were to flow from the success of the enterprise, must have been considered sublime.

The splendidly decorated ship which Matilda had presented to her husband proved itself, on trial, to be something more than a mere toy. It led the van at the commencement, of course; and as all eyes watched its progress, it soon became evident that it was slowly gaining upon the rest of the squadron, so as continually to increase its distance from those that were following it. William, pleased with the success of its performance, ordered the sailing master to keep on, without regard to those who were behind; and thus it happened that, when night came on, the fleet was at very considerable distance in rear of the flag ship.

Of course, under these circumstances, the fleet disappeared from sight when the sun went down, but all expected that it would come into view again in the morning. When the morning came, however, to the surprise and disappointment of every one on board the flag ship, no signs of the fleet were to be seen. The seamen, and the officers on the deck, gazed long and intently into the southern horizon as the increasing light of the morning brought it gradually into view, but there was not a speck to break its smooth and even line.

They felt anxious and uneasy, but William seemed to experience no concern. He ordered the sails to be furled, and then sent a man to the mast head to look out there. Nothing was to be seen. William, still apparently unconcerned, ordered breakfast to be prepared in a very sumptuous manner, loading the tables with wine and other delicacies, that the minds of all on board might be cheered by the exhilarating influence of a feast. At length the lookout was sent to the mast head again. "What do you see now?" said William. "I see," said the man, gazing very intently all the while toward the south, "four *very small specks* just in the horizon." The intense interest which this announcement awakened on the deck was soon at the same time *heightened* and *relieved* by the cry, "I can see more and more—they are the ships—yes, the whole squadron is coming into view."

The advancing fleet soon came up with the Mira, when the latter spread her sails again, and all moved slowly on together toward the coast of England.

The ships had directed their course so much to the eastward, that when they made the land they were not very far from the Straits of Dover. As they drew near to the English shore, they watched very narrowly for the appearance of Harold's cruisers, which they naturally expected would have been stationed at various points, to guard the coast; but none were to be seen. There had been such cruisers, and there still were such off the other harbors; but it happened, very fortunately for William, that those which had been stationed to guard this part of the island had been withdrawn a few days before, on account of their provisions being exhausted. Thus, when William's fleet arrived, there was no enemy to oppose their landing. There was a large and open bay, called the Bay of Pevensey, which lay smiling before them, extending its arms as if inviting them in. The fleet advanced to within the proper distance from the land, and there the seamen cast their anchors, and all began to prepare for the work of disembarkation.

A strong body of soldiery is of course landed first on such occasions. In this instance the archers, William's favorite corps, were selected to take the lead. William accompanied them. In his eagerness to get to the shore, as he leaped from the boat, his foot slipped, and he fell. The officers and men around him would have considered this an evil omen; but he had presence of mind enough to extend his arms and grasp the ground, pretending that his prostration was designed, and saying at the same time, "Thus I seize this land; from this moment it is mine." As he arose, one of his officers ran to a neighboring hut which stood near by upon the shore, and breaking off a little of the thatch, carried it to William, and, putting it into his hand, said that he thus gave him *seizin* of his new possessions. This was a customary form, in those times, of putting a new owner into possession of lands which he had purchased or acquired in any other way. The new proprietor would repair to the ground, where the party whose province it was to deliver the property would detach something from it, such as a piece of turf from a bank, or a little of the thatch from a cottage, and offering it to him, would say, "Thus I deliver thee *seizin*," that is, *possession*, "of this land." This ceremony was necessary to complete the conveyance of the estate.

The soldiers, as soon as they were landed, began immediately to form an encampment, and to make such military arrangements as were necessary to guard against an attack, or the sudden appearance of an enemy. While this was going on, the boats continued to pass to and fro, accomplishing, as fast as possible, the work of disembarkation. In addition to those regularly attached to the army, there was a vast company of workmen of all kinds, engineers, pioneers, carpenters, masons, and laborers, to be landed; and there were three towers, or rather forts, built of timber, which had been framed and fashioned in Normandy, ready to be put up on arriving: these had now to be landed, piece by piece, on the strand. These forts were to be erected as soon as the army should have chosen a position for a permanent encampment, and were intended as a means of protection for the provisions and stores. The circumstance shows that the plan of transporting buildings ready made, across the seas, has not been invented anew by our emigrants to California.

While these operations were going on, William dispatched small squadrons of horse as reconnoitering parties, to explore the country around, to see if there were any indications that Harold was near. These parties returned, one after another, after having gone some miles into the country in all directions, and reported that there were no signs of an enemy to be seen. Things were now getting settled, too, in the camp, and William gave directions that the army should kindle their camp fires for the night, and prepare and eat their suppers. His own supper, or dinner, as perhaps it might be called, was also served, which he partook, with his officers, in his own tent. His mind was in a state of great contentment and satisfaction at the successful accomplishment of the landing, and at finding himself thus safely established, at the head of a vast force, within the realm of England.

Every circumstance of the transit had been favorable excepting one, and that was, that two of the ships belonging to the fleet were missing. William inquired at supper if any tidings of them had been received. They told him, in reply, that the missing vessels had been heard from; they had, in some way or other, been run upon the rocks and lost. There was a certain astrologer, who had made a great parade, before the expedition left Normandy, of predicting its result. He had found, by consulting the stars, that William would be successful, and would meet with no opposition from Harold. This astrologer had been on board one of the missing ships, and was drowned. William remarked, on receiving this information, "What an idiot a man must be, to think that he can predict, by means of the stars, the future fate of others, when it is so plain that he can not foresee his own!"

It is said that William's dinner on this occasion was served on a large stone instead of a table. The stone still remains on the spot, and is called "the Conqueror's Stone" to this day.

The next day after the landing, the army was put in motion, and advanced along the coast toward the eastward. There was no armed enemy to contend against them there or to oppose their march; the people of the country, through which the army moved, far from attempting to resist them, were filled with terror and dismay. This terror was heightened, in fact, by some excesses of which some parties of the soldiers were guilty. The inhabitants of the hamlets and villages, overwhelmed with consternation at the sudden descent upon their shores of such a vast horde of wild and desperate foreigners, fled in all directions. Some made their escape into the interior; others, taking with them the helpless members of their households, and such valuables as they could carry, sought refuge in monasteries and churches, supposing that such sanctuaries as those, not even soldiers, unless they were pagans, would dare to violate. Others, still, attempted to conceal themselves in thickets and fens till the vast throng which was sweeping onward like a tornado should have passed. Though William afterward always evinced a decided disposition to protect the peaceful inhabitants of the country from all aggressions on the part of his troops, he had no time to attend to that subject now. He was intent on pressing forward to a place of safety.

William reached at length a position which seemed to him suitable for a permanent encampment. It was an elevated land, near the sea. To the westward of it was a valley formed by a sort of recess opened in the range of chalky cliffs which here form the shore of England. In the bottom of this valley, down upon the beach, was a small town, then of no great consequence or power, but whose name, which was Hastings, has since been immortalized by the battle which was fought in its vicinity a few days after William's arrival. The position which William selected for his encampment was on high land in the vicinity of the town. The lines of the encampment were marked out, and the forts or castles which had been brought from Normandy were set up within the inclosures. Vast multitudes of laborers were soon at work, throwing up embankments, and building redoubts and bastions, while others were transporting the arms, the provisions, and the munitions of war, and storing them in security within the lines. The encampment was soon completed, and the long line of tents were set up in streets and squares within it. By the time, however, that the work was done, some of William's agents and spies came into camp from the north, saying that in four days Harold would be upon him at the head of a hundred thousand men.

10

The Battle of Hastings

A.D. 1066

Tostig.—He is driven from England.—Expedition of Tostig.—He sails to Norway.—Tostig's alliance with the Norwegians.—The Norwegian fleet. —Superstitions.—Dreams of the soldiers.—The combined fleets.—Attack on Scarborough.—The rolling fire.—Burning of Scarborough.—Tostig marches to York.—Surrender of the city.—Arrival of King Harold.— Movements of Tostig.—Surprise of Tostig and his allies.—Preparations for battle.—Negotiations between Tostig and his brother.—The battle.— Death of Tostig.—The Norwegians retire.—Harold attempts to surprise William.—His failure.—Advice of Harold's counselors.—He rejects it.— Harold's encampment.—The country alarmed.—Harold's brothers.—He proposes to visit William's camp.—Harold's arrival at William's lines. —He reconnoiters the camp.—Harold's despondency.—His spies.—Their report.—William's ambassadors.—Their propositions.—William's propositions unreasonable.—Harold declines them.—Further proposals of William.—Counter proposal of Harold.—Harold's forebodings.—Proposals of his brothers.—Night before the battle.—Scenes in Harold's camp.— Scenes in William's camp.—Religious ceremonies.—A martial bishop.— William's war-horse.—Preliminary arrangements.—Battle of Hastings. —Defeat of Harold.—He is slain.—Final subjugation of the island.— William crowned at Westminster.—William's power.—His greatness.

THE reader will doubtless recollect that the tidings which William first received of the accession of King Harold were brought to him by Tostig, Harold's brother, on the day when he was trying his bow and arrows in the park at Rouen. Tostig was his brother's most inveterate foe. He had been, during the reign of Edward, a great chieftain, ruling over the north of England. The city of York was then his capital. He had been expelled from these his dominions, and had quarreled with his brother Harold in respect to his right to be restored to them. In the course of this quarrel he was driven from the country altogether, and went to the Continent, burning with rage and resentment against his brother; and when he came to inform William of Harold's usurpation, his object was not merely to arouse *William* to action—he wished to act himself. He told William that he himself had more influence in England still than his brother, and that if William would supply him with a small fleet and a moderate number of men, he would make a descent upon the coast and show what he could do.

William acceded to his proposal, and furnished him with the force which he required, and Tostig set sail. William had not, apparently, much confidence in the power of Tostig to produce any great effect, but his efforts, he thought, might cause some alarm in England, and occasion sudden and fatiguing marches to the troops, and thus distract and weaken King Harold's forces. William would not, therefore, accompany Tostig himself, but, dismissing him with such force as he could readily raise on so sudden a call, he remained himself in Normandy, and commenced in earnest his own grand preparations, as is described in the last chapter.

Tostig did not think it prudent to attempt a landing on English shores until he had obtained some accession to the force which William had given him. He accordingly passed through the Straits of Dover, and then turning northward, he sailed along the eastern shores of the German Ocean in search of allies. He came, at length, to Norway. He entered into negotiations there with the Norwegian king, whose name, too, was Harold. This northern Harold was a wild and adventurous soldier and sailor, a sort of sea king, who had spent a considerable portion of his life in marauding excursions upon the seas. He readily entered into Tostig's views. An arrangement was soon concluded, and Tostig set sail again to cross the German Ocean toward the British shores, while Harold promised to collect and equip his own fleet as soon as possible, and follow him. All this took place early in September; so that, at the same time that William's threatened invasion was gathering strength and menacing Harold's southern frontier, a cloud equally dark and gloomy, and quite as threatening in its aspect, was rising and swelling in the north; while King Harold himself, though full of vague uneasiness and alarm, could gain no certain information in respect to either of these dangers.

The Norwegian fleet assembled at the port appointed for the rendezvous of it, but, as the season was advanced and the weather stormy, the soldiers there, like William's soldiers on the coast of France, were afraid to put to sea. Some of them had dreams which they considered as bad omens; and so much superstitious importance was attached to such ideas in those times that these dreams were gravely recorded by the writers of the ancient chronicles, and have come down to us as part of the regular and sober history of the times. One soldier dreamed that the expedition had sailed and landed on the English coast, and that there the English army came out to meet them. Before the front of the army rode a woman of gigantic stature, mounted on a wolf. The wolf had in his jaws a human body, dripping with blood, which he was engaged in devouring as he came along. The woman gave the wolf another victim after he had devoured the first.

Another of these ominous dreams was the following: Just as the fleet was about setting sail, the dreamer saw a crowd of ravenous vultures and birds of prey come and alight everywhere upon the sails and rigging of the ships, as if they were going to accompany the expedition. Upon the summit of a rock near the shore there sat the figure of a female, with a stern and ferocious countenance, and a drawn sword in her hand. She was busy counting the ships, pointing at them, as she counted, with her sword. She seemed a sort of fiend of destruction, and she called out to the birds, to encourage them to go. "Go!" said she, "without fear; you shall have abundance of prey. I am going too."

It is obvious that these dreams might as easily have been interpreted to portend death and destruction to their English foes as to the dreamers themselves. The soldiers were, however, inclined—in the state of mind which the season of the year, the threatening aspect of the skies, and the certain dangers of their distant expedition, produced—to apply the gloomy predictions which they imagined these dreams expressed, to themselves. Their chief, however, was of too desperate and determined a character to pay any regard to such influences. He set sail. His armament crossed the German Sea in safety, and joined Tostig on the coast of Scotland. The combined fleet moved slowly southward, along the shore, watching for an opportunity to land.

The Norwegians at Scarborough

They reached, at length, the town of Scarborough, and landed to attack it. The inhabitants retired within the walls, shut the gates, and bid the invaders defiance. The town was situated under a hill, which rose in a steep acclivity upon one side. The story is, that the Norwegians went upon this hill, where they piled up an enormous heap of trunks and branches of trees, with the interstices filled with stubble, dried bark, and roots, and other such combustibles, and then setting the whole mass on fire, they rolled it down into the town—a vast ball of fire, roaring and crackling more and more, by the fanning of its flames in the wind, as it bounded along. The intelligent reader will, of course, pause and hesitate, in considering how far to credit such a story. It is obviously impossible that any mere *pile*, however closely packed, could be made to roll. But it is, perhaps, not absolutely impossible that trunks of trees might be framed together, or fastened with wet thongs or iron chains, after being made in the form of a rude cylinder or ball, and filled with combustibles within, so as to retain its integrity in such a descent.

The account states that this strange method of bombardment was successful. The town was set on fire; the people surrendered. Tostig and the Norwegians plundered it, and then, embarking again in their ships, they continued their voyage.

The intelligence of this descent upon his northern coasts reached Harold in London toward the close of September, just as he was withdrawing his forces from the southern frontier, as was related in the last chapter, under the idea that the Norman invasion would probably be postponed until the spring; so that, instead of sending his troops into their winter quarters, he had to concentrate them again with all dispatch, and march at the head of them to the north, to avert this new and unexpected danger.

While King Harold was thus advancing to meet them, Tostig and his Norwegian allies entered the River Humber. Their object was to reach the city of York, which had been Tostig's former capital, and which was situated near the River Ouse, a branch of the Humber. They accordingly ascended the Humber to the mouth of the Ouse, and thence up the latter river to a suitable point of debarkation not far from York. Here they landed and formed a great encampment. From this encampment they advanced to the siege of the city. The inhabitants made some resistance at first; but, finding that their cause was hopeless, they offered to surrender, and a treaty of surrender was finally concluded. This negotiation was closed toward the evening of the day, and Tostig and his confederate forces were to be admitted on the morrow. They therefore, feeling that their prize was secure, withdrew to their encampment for the night, and left the city to its repose.

It so happened that King Harold arrived that very night, coming to the rescue of the city. He expected to have found an army of besiegers around the walls, but, instead of that, there was nothing to intercept his progress up to the very gates of the city. The inhabitants opened the gates to receive him, and the whole detachment which was marching under his command passed in, while Tostig and his Norwegian allies were sleeping quietly in their camp, wholly unconscious of the great change which had thus taken place in the situation of their affairs.

The next morning Tostig drew out a large portion of the army, and formed them in array, for the purpose of advancing to take possession of the city. Although it was September, and the weather had been cold and stormy, it happened that, on that morning, the sun came out bright, and the air was calm, giving promise of a warm day; and as the movement into the city was to be a peaceful one—a procession, as it were, and not a hostile march—the men were ordered to leave their coats of mail and all their heavy armor in camp, that they might march the more unencumbered. While they were advancing in this unconcerned and almost defenseless condition, they saw before them, on the road leading to the city, a great cloud of dust arising. It was a strong body of King Harold's troops coming out to attack them. At first, Tostig and the Norwegians were completely lost and bewildered at the appearance of so unexpected a spectacle. Very soon they could see weapons glittering here and there, and banners flying. A cry of "The enemy! the enemy!" arose, and passed along their ranks, producing universal alarm. Tostig and the Norwegian Harold halted their men, and marshaled them hastily in battle array. The English Harold did the same, when he had drawn up near to the front of the enemy; both parties then paused, and stood surveying one another. Presently there was seen advancing from the English side a squadron of twenty horsemen, splendidly armed, and bearing a flag of truce. They approached to within a short distance of the Norwegian lines, when a herald, who was among them, called out aloud for Tostig. Tostig came forward in answer to the summons. The herald then proclaimed to Tostig that his brother did not wish to contend with him, but desired, on the contrary, that they should live together in harmony. He offered him peace, therefore, if he would lay down his arms, and he promised to restore him his former possessions and honors.

Tostig seemed very much inclined to receive this proposition favorably. He paused and hesitated. At length he asked the messenger what terms King Harold would make with his friend and ally, the Norwegian Harold. "He shall have," replied the messenger, "seven feet of English ground for a grave. He shall have a little more than that, for he is taller than common men." "Then," replied Tostig, "tell my brother to prepare for battle. It shall never be said that I abandoned and betrayed my ally and friend."

The troop returned with Tostig's answer to Harold's lines, and the battle almost immediately began. Of course the most eager and inveterate hostility of the English army would be directed against the Norwegians and their king, whom they considered as foreign intruders, without any excuse or pretext for their aggression. It accordingly happened that, very soon after the commencement of the conflict, Harold the Norwegian fell, mortally wounded by an arrow in his throat. The English king then made new proposals to Tostig to cease the combat, and come to some terms of accommodation. But, in the meantime, Tostig had become himself incensed, and would listen to no overtures of peace. He continued the combat until he was himself killed. The remaining combatants in his army had now no longer any motive for resistance. Harold offered them a free passage to their ships, that they might return home in peace, if they would lay down their arms. They accepted the offer, retired on board their ships, and set sail. Harold then, having, in the meantime, heard of William's landing on the southern coast, set out on his return to the southward, to meet the more formidable enemy that menaced him there.

His army, though victorious, was weakened by the fatigues of the march, and by the losses suffered in the battle. Harold himself had been wounded, though not so severely as to prevent his continuing to exercise the command. He pressed on toward the south with great energy, sending messages on every side, into the surrounding country, on his line of march, calling upon the chieftains to arm themselves and their followers, and to come on with all possible dispatch, and join him. He hoped to advance so rapidly to the southern coast as to surprise William before he should have fully intrenched himself in his camp, and without his being aware of his enemy's approach. But William, in order to guard effectually against surprise, had sent out small reconnoitering parties of horsemen on all the roads leading northward, that they might bring him in intelligence of the first approach of the enemy. Harold's advanced guard met these parties, and saw them as they drove rapidly back to the camp to give the alarm. Thus the hope of surprising William was disappointed. Harold found, too, by his spies, as he drew near, to his utter dismay, that William's forces were four times as numerous as his own. It would, of course, be madness for him to think of attacking an enemy in his intrenchments with such an inferior force. The only alternative left him was either to retreat, or else to take some strong position and fortify himself there, in the hope of being able to resist the invaders and arrest their advance, though he was not strong enough to attack them.

Some of his counselors advised him not to hazard a battle at all, but to fall back toward London, carrying with him or destroying everything which could afford sustenance to William's army from the whole breadth of the land. This would soon, they said, reduce William's army to great distress for want of food, since it would be impossible for him to transport supplies across the Channel for so vast a multitude. Besides, they said, this plan would compel William, in the extremity to which he would be reduced, to make so many predatory excursions among the more distant villages and towns, as would exasperate the inhabitants, and induce them to join Harold's army in great numbers to repel the invasion. Harold listened to these counsels, but said, after consideration, that he could never adopt such a plan. He could not be so derelict to his duty as to lay waste a country which he was under obligations to protect and save, or compel his people to come to his aid by exposing them, designedly, to the excesses and cruelties of so ferocious an enemy.

Harold determined, therefore, on giving William battle. It was not necessary, however, for him to attack the invader. He perceived at once that if he should take a strong position and fortify himself in it, William must necessarily attack *him*, since a foreign army, just landed in the country, could not long remain inactive on the shore. Harold accordingly chose a position six or seven miles from William's camp, and fortified himself strongly there. Of course neither army was in sight of the other, or knew the numbers, disposition, or plans of the enemy. The country between them was, so far as the inhabitants were concerned, a scene of consternation and terror. No one knew at what point the two vast clouds of danger and destruction which were hovering near them would meet, or over what regions the terrible storm which was to burst forth when the hour of that meeting should come, would sweep in its destructive fury. The inhabitants, therefore, were every where flying in dismay, conveying away the aged and the helpless by any means which came most readily to hand; taking with them, too, such treasures as they could carry, and hiding, in rude and uncertain places of concealment, those which they were compelled to leave behind. The region, thus, which lay between the two encampments was rapidly becoming a solitude and a desolation, across which no communication was made, and no tidings passed to give the armies at the encampments intelligence of each other.

Harold had two brothers among the officers of his army, Gurth and Leofwin. Their conduct toward the king seems to have been of a more fraternal character than that of Tostig, who had acted the part of a rebel and an enemy. Gurth and Leofwin, on the contrary, adhered to his cause, and, as the hour of danger and the great crisis which was to decide their fate drew nigh, they kept close to his side, and evinced a truly fraternal solicitude for his safety. It was they, specially, who had recommended to Harold to fall back on London, and not risk his life, and the fate of his kingdom, on the uncertain event of a battle.

As soon as Harold had completed his encampment, he expressed a desire to Gurth to ride across the intermediate country and take a view of William's lines. Such an undertaking was less dangerous then than it would be at the present day; for now, such a reconnoitering party would be discovered from the enemy's encampment, at a great distance, by means of spy-glasses, and a twenty-four-pound shot or a shell would be sent from a battery to blow the party to pieces or drive them away. The only danger *then* was of being pursued by a detachment of horsemen from the camp, or surrounded by an ambuscade. To guard against these dangers, Harold and Gurth took the most powerful and fleetest horses in the camp, and they called out a small but strong guard of well-selected men to escort them. Thus provided and attended, they rode over to the enemy's lines, and advanced so near that, from a small eminence to which they ascended, they could survey the whole scene of William's encampment: the palisades and embankments with which it was guarded, which extended for miles; the long lines of tents within; the vast multitude of soldiers; the knights and officers riding to and fro, glittering with steel; and the grand pavilion of the duke himself, with the consecrated banner of the cross floating above it. Harold was very much impressed with the grandeur of the spectacle.

After gazing on this scene for some time in silence, Harold said to Gurth that perhaps, after all, the policy of falling back would have been the wisest for them to adopt, rather than to risk a battle with so overwhelming a force as they saw before them. He did not know, he added, but that it would be best for them to change their plan, and adopt that policy now. Gurth said that it was too late. They had taken their stand, and now for them to break up their encampment and retire would be considered a retreat and not a maneuver, and it would discourage and dishearten the whole realm.

After surveying thus, as long as they desired to do so, the situation and extent of William's encampment, Harold's party returned to their own lines, still determined to make a stand there against the invaders, but feeling great doubt and despondency in respect to the result. Harold sent over, too, in the course of the day, some spies. The men whom he employed for this purpose were Normans by birth, and they could speak the French language. There were many Normans in England, who had come over in King Edward's time. These Norman spies could, of course, disguise themselves, and mingle, without attracting attention, among the thousands of workmen and camp followers that were going and coming continually around the grounds which William's army occupied. They did this so effectually, that they penetrated within the encampment without difficulty, examined everything, and, in due time, returned to Harold with their report. They gave a formidable account of the numbers and condition of William's troops. There was a large corps of bowmen in the army, which had adopted a fashion of being shaven and shorn in such a manner that the spies mistook them for priests. They told Harold, accordingly, on their return, that there were more *priests* in William's camp than there were soldiers in all his army.

During this eventful day, William too sent a body of horsemen across the country which separated the two encampments, though his emissaries were not spies, but ambassadors, with propositions for peace. William had no wish to fight a battle, if what he considered as rightfully his kingdom could be delivered to him without it; and he determined to make one final effort to obtain a peaceable surrender of it, before coming to the dreadful resort of an appeal to arms. He accordingly sent his embassy with *three* propositions to make to the English king. The principal messenger in this company was a monk, whose name was Maigrot. He rode, with a proper escort and a flag of truce, to Harold's lines. The propositions were these, by accepting either of which the monk said that Harold might avoid a battle. 1. That Harold should surrender the kingdom to William, as he had solemnly sworn to do over the sacred relics in Normandy. 2. That they should both agree to refer the whole subject of controversy between them to the pope, and abide by his decision. 3. That they should settle the dispute by single combat, the two claimants to the crown to fight a duel on the plain, in presence of their respective armies.

It is obvious that Harold could not accept either of these propositions. The first was to give up the whole point at issue. As for the second, the pope had already prejudged the case, and if it were to be referred to him, there could be no doubt that he would simply reaffirm his former decision. And in respect to single combat, the disadvantage on Harold's part would be as great in such a contest as it would be in the proposed arbitration. He was himself a man of comparatively slender form and of little bodily strength. William, on the other hand, was distinguished for his size, and for his extraordinary muscular energy. In a modern combat with firearms these personal advantages would be of no avail, but in those days, when the weapons were battle-axes, lances, and swords, they were almost decisive of the result. Harold therefore declined all William's propositions, and the monk returned.

William seems not to have been wholly discouraged by this failure of his first attempt at negotiation, for he sent his embassage a second time to make one more proposal. It was, that if Harold would consent to acknowledge William as King of England, William would assign the whole territory to him and to his brother Gurth, to hold *as provinces*, under William's general sway. Under this arrangement William would himself return to Normandy, making the city of Rouen, which was his capital there, the capital of the whole united realm. To this proposal Harold replied, that he could not, on any terms, give up his rights as sovereign of England. He therefore declined this proposal also. He, however, now made a proposition in his turn. He was willing, he said, to compromise the dispute, so far as it could be done by *the payment of money*. If William would abandon his invasion and return to Normandy, giving up his claims to the English crown, he would pay him, he said, any sum of money that he would name.

William could not accept this proposal. He was, as he believed, the true and rightful heir to the throne of England, and there was a point of honor involved, as well as a dictate of ambition to be obeyed, in insisting on the claim. In the mean time, the day had passed, while these fruitless negotiations had been pending. Night was coming on. William's officers and counselors began to be uneasy at the delay. They said that every hour new re-enforcements were coming into Harold's camp, while they themselves were gaining no advantage, and, consequently, the longer the battle was delayed, the less was the certainty of victory. So William promised them that he would attack King Harold in his camp the very next morning.

As the time for the great final struggle drew near, Harold's mind was oppressed more and more with a sense of anxiety and with foreboding fears. His brothers, too, were ill at ease. Their solicitude was increased by the recollection of Harold's oath, and of the awful sanctions with which they feared the sacred relics might have invested it. They were not sure that their brother's excuse for setting it aside would save him from the guilt and curse of perjury in the sight of Heaven. So they proposed, on the eve of the battle, that Harold himself should retire, and leave them to conduct the defense. "We can not deny," they said, "that you did take the oath; and, notwithstanding the circumstances which seem to absolve you from the obligation, it is best to avoid, if possible, the open violation of it. It will be better, on the whole, for you to leave the army and go to London. You can aid very effectually in the defense of the kingdom by raising re-enforcements there. We will stay and encounter the actual battle. Heaven can not be displeased with us for so doing, for we shall be only discharging the duty incumbent on all, of defending their native land from foreign invasion."

Harold would not consent to adopt this plan. He could not retire himself, he said, at the hour of approaching danger, and leave his brothers and his friends exposed, when it was *his* crown for which they were contending.

Such were the circumstances of the two armies on the evening before the battle; and, of course, in such a state of things, the tendency of the minds of men would be, in Harold's camp, to gloom and despondency, and in William's, to confidence and exultation. Harold undertook, as men in his circumstances often do, to lighten the load which weighed upon his own heart and oppressed the spirits of his men, by feasting and wine. He ordered a plentiful supper to be served, and supplied his soldiers with abundance of drink; and it is said that his whole camp exhibited, during the whole night, one wide-spread scene of carousing and revelry, the troops being gathered every where in groups around their camp fires, some half stupefied, others quarreling, and others still singing national songs, and dancing with wild excitement, according to the various effects produced upon different constitutions by the intoxicating influence of beer and wine.

In William's camp there were witnessed very different scenes. There were a great many monks and ecclesiastics in the train of his army, and, on the night before the battle, they spent the time in saying masses, reading litanies and prayers, chanting anthems, and in other similar acts of worship, assisted by the soldiers, who gathered, in great congregations, for this wild worship, in the open spaces among the tents and around the campfires. At length they all retired to rest, feeling an additional sense of safety in respect to the work of the morrow by having, as they supposed, entitled themselves, by their piety, to the protection of Heaven.

In the morning, too, in William's camp, the first thing done was to convene the army for a grand celebration of mass. It is a curious illustration of the mingling of the religious, or, perhaps, we ought rather to say, the superstitious sentiment of the times, with the spirit of war, that the bishop who officiated in this solemn service of the mass wore a coat of mail under his pontifical attire, and an attendant stood by his side, while he was offering his prayers, with a steel-pointed spear in his hand, ready for the martial prelate to assume as soon as the service should be ended. Accordingly, when the religious duty was performed, the bishop threw off his surplice, took his spear, and mounting his white charger, which was also all saddled and bridled beside him, he headed a brigade of horse, and rode on to the assault of the enemy.

William himself mounted a very magnificent war-horse from Spain, a present which he had formerly received from one of his wealthy barons. The name of the horse was Bayard. From William's neck were suspended some of the most sacred of the relics over which Harold had taken his false oath. He imagined that there would be some sort of charm in them, to protect his life, and to make the judgment of Heaven more sure against the perjurer. The standard which the pope had blessed was borne by his side by a young standard bearer, who was very proud of the honor. An older soldier, however, on whom the care of this standard officially devolved, had asked to be excused from carrying it. He wished, he said, to do his work that day with the *sword*. While making these preliminary arrangements for going into battle, William, with the party around him, stood upon a gentle eminence in the middle of the camp, and in sight of the whole army. Everyone was struck with admiration at the splendid figure which their commander made—his large and well-formed limbs covered with steel, and his horse, whose form was as noble as that of his master, prancing restlessly, as if impatient for the battle to begin.

When all were ready, the Norman army advanced gayly and joyously to attack the English lines; but the gayety and joyousness of the scene soon disappeared, as corps after corps got fairly engaged in the awful work of the day. For ten long hours there reigned over the whole field one wide-spread scene of havoc and death—every soul among all those countless thousands delivered up to the supreme dominion of the most dreadful passions, excited to a perfect phrensy of hatred, rage, and revenge, and all either mercilessly killing others, or dying themselves in agony and despair. When night came, the Normans were every where victorious. They were in full possession of the field, and they rode triumphantly to and fro through Harold's camp, leaping their horses over the bodies of the dead and dying which covered the ground. Those of

King Harold's followers that had escaped the slaughter of the day fled in hopeless confusion toward the north, where the flying masses strewed the roads for miles with the bodies of men who sank down on the way, spent with wounds or exhausted by fatigue.

In the morning, William marshaled his men on the field, and called over the names of the officers and men, as they had been registered in Normandy, for the purpose of ascertaining who were killed. While this melancholy ceremony was going on, two monks came in, sent from the remains of the English army, and saying that King Harold was missing, and that it was rumored that he had been slain. If so, his body must be lying somewhere, they said, upon the field, and they wished for permission to make search for it. The permission was granted. With the aid of some soldiers they began to explore the ground, turning over and examining every lifeless form which, by the dress or the armor, might seem to be possibly the king's. Their search was for a long time vain; the ghastly faces of the dead were so mutilated and changed that nobody could be identified. At length, however, a woman who had been in Harold's family, and knew his person more intimately than they, found and recognized the body, and the monks and the soldiers carried it away.

* * *

The battle of Hastings sealed and settled the controversy in respect to the English crown. It is true that the adherents of Harold, and also those of Edgar Atheling, made afterward various efforts to rally their forces and recover the kingdom, but in vain. William advanced to London, fortified himself there, and made excursions from that city as a centre until he reduced the island to his sway. He was crowned at length, at Westminster Abbey, with great pomp and parade. He sent for Matilda to come and join him, and instated her in his palace as Queen of England. He confiscated the property of all the English nobles who had fought against him, and divided it among the Norman chieftains who had aided him in the invasion. He made various excursions to and from Normandy himself, being received everywhere throughout his dominions, on both sides the Channel, with the most distinguished honors. In a word, he became, in the course of a few years after he landed, one of the greatest and most powerful potentates on the globe. How far all his riches and grandeur were from making him happy, will appear in the following chapter.

11

Prince Robert's Rebellion

A.D. 1076-1077

William's oldest son.—His character.—William's conflicts with his son Robert.—William Rufus.—William's son Henry.—Robert nicknamed Short Boots.—Robert's betrothment.—William's motives.—Death of Margaret.—More trouble.—Robert's political power.—His ambition.—Robert claims Normandy.—William refuses it.—Castle at L'Aigle.—Quarrel between Robert and William Rufus.—The combatants parted. —Robert's rage.—Robert's rebellion.—Anxiety and distress of Matilda. —Measures of Matilda.—Advantages of William.—Robert lays down his arms.—Interview with his father.—Recriminations.—The interview fruitless.—Robert goes to Flanders.—His treasonable correspondence.— Action of Philip.—He sides with Robert.—Robert's dissipation.—Matilda sends him supplies.—Matilda's secret supplies.—She is discovered.— Matilda's messenger seized.—William's reproaches.—Matilda's reply. —William's anger.—Sampson's escape.—Things grow worse.—Preparations for war.—Matilda's distress.—William wounded by his son.—The battle goes against him.—Matilda's anguish.—The reconciliation.

AMBITIOUS men, who devote their time and attention, through all the early years of life, to their personal and political aggrandizement, have little time to appropriate to the government and education of their children, and their later years are often embittered by the dissipation and vice, or by the unreasonable exactions of their sons. At least it was so in William's case. By the time that his public enemies were subdued, and he found himself undisputed master both of his kingdom and his duchy, his peace and happiness were destroyed, and the tranquillity of his whole realm was disturbed by a terrible family quarrel.

The name of his oldest son was Robert. He was fourteen years old when his father set off on his invasion of England. At that time he was a sort of spoiled child, having been his mother's favorite, and, as such, always greatly indulged by her. When William went away, it will be recollected that he appointed Matilda regent, to govern Normandy during his absence. This boy was also named in the regency, so that he was nominally associated with his mother, and he considered himself, doubtless, as the more important personage of the two. In a word, while William was engaged in England, prosecuting his conquests there, Robert was growing up in Normandy a vain, self-conceited, and ungovernable young man.

His father, in going back and forth between England and Normandy, often came into conflict with his son, as usual in such cases. In these contests Matilda took sides with the son. William's second son, whose name was William Rufus, was jealous of his older brother, and was often provoked by the overbearing and imperious spirit which Robert displayed. William Rufus thus naturally adhered to the father's part in the family feud. William Rufus was as rough and turbulent in spirit as Robert, but he had not been so indulged. He possessed, therefore, more self-control; he knew very well how to suppress his propensities, and conceal the unfavorable aspects of his character when in the presence of his father.

There was a third brother, named Henry. He was of a more quiet and inoffensive character, and avoided taking an active part in the quarrel, except so far as William Rufus led him on. He was William Rufus's friend and companion, and, as such, Robert considered him as his enemy. All, in fact, except Matilda, were against Robert, who looked down, in a haughty and domineering manner—as the oldest son and heir is very apt to do in rich and powerful families—upon the comparative insignificance of his younger brethren. The king, instead of restraining this imperious spirit in his son, as he might, perhaps, have done by a considerate and kind, and, at the same time, decisive exercise of authority, teased and tormented him by sarcasms and petty vexations. Among other instances of this, he gave him the nickname of *Short Boots*, because he was of inferior stature. As Robert was, however, at this time of full age, he was stung to the quick at having such a stigma attached to him by his father, and his bosom burned with secret sentiments of resentment and revenge.

He had, besides, other causes of complaint against his father, more serious still. When he was a very young child, his father, according to the custom of the times, had espoused him to the daughter and heiress of a neighboring earl, a child like himself. Her name was Margaret. The earldom which this little Margaret was to inherit was Maine. It was on the frontiers of Normandy, and it was a rich and valuable possession. It was a part of the stipulation of the marriage contract that the young bride's domain was to be delivered to the father of the bridegroom, to be held by him until the bridegroom should become of age, and the marriage should be fully consummated. In fact, the getting possession of this rich inheritance, with a prospect of holding it so many years, was very probably the principal end which William had in view in contracting for a matrimonial union so very premature.

If this was, in reality, William's plan, it resulted, in the end, even more favorably than he had anticipated; for the little heiress died a short time after her inheritance was put into the possession of her father-in-law. There was nobody to demand a restoration of it, and so William continued to hold it until his son, the bridegroom, became of age. Robert then demanded it, contending that it was justly his. William refused to surrender it. He maintained that what had passed between his son in his infancy, and the little Margaret, was not a marriage, but only a betrothment—a contract for a future marriage, which was to take place when the parties were of age—that, since Margaret's death prevented the consummation of the union, Robert was never her husband, and could not, consequently, acquire the rights of a husband. The lands, therefore, ought manifestly, he said, to remain in the hands of her guardian, and whatever rights any other persons might have, claiming to succeed Margaret as her natural heirs, it was plain that his son could have no title whatever.

However satisfactory this reasoning might be to the mind of William, Robert was only exasperated by it. He looked upon the case as one of extreme injustice and oppression on the part of his father, who, not content, he said, with his own enormous possessions, must add to them by robbing his own son. In this opinion Robert's mother, Matilda, agreed with him. As for William Rufus and Henry, they paid little attention to the argument, but were pleased with the result of it, and highly enjoyed their brother's vexation and chagrin in not being able to get possession of his earldom.

There was another very serious subject of dispute between Robert and his father. It has already been stated, that when the duke set out on his expedition for the invasion of England, he left Matilda and Robert together in charge of the duchy. At the commencement of the period of his absence Robert was very young, and the actual power rested mainly in his mother's hands. As he grew older, however, he began to exercise an increasing influence and control. In fact, as he was himself ambitious and aspiring, and his mother indulgent, the power passed very rapidly into his hands. It was eight years from the time that William left Normandy before his power was so far settled and established in England that he could again take the affairs of his original realm into his hands. He had left Robert, at that time, a mere boy of fourteen, who, though rude and turbulent in character, was still politically powerless. He found him, on his return, a man of twenty-two, ruder and more turbulent than before, and in the full possession of political power. This power, too, he found him very unwilling to surrender.

In fact, when William came to receive back the province of Normandy again, Robert almost refused to surrender it. He said that his father had always promised him the duchy of Normandy as his domain so soon as he should become of age, and he claimed now the fulfillment of this promise. Besides, he said that, now that his father was King of England, his former realm was of no consequence to him. It did not add sensibly to his influence or his power, and he might, therefore, without suffering any sensible loss himself, grant it to his son. William, on his part, did not acknowledge the force of either of these arguments. He would not admit that he had ever promised Normandy to his son; and as to voluntarily relinquishing any part of his possessions, he had no faith in the policy of a man's giving up his power or his property to his children until they were justly entitled to inherit it by his death; at any rate, he should not do it. He had no idea, as he expressed it, "of putting off his clothes before he was going to bed."

The irritation and ill-will which these dissensions produced grew deeper and more inveterate every day, though the disagreement had been thus far a private and domestic dispute, confined, in its influence, to the king's immediate household. An occasion, however, now occurred, on which the private family feud broke out into an open public quarrel. The circumstances were these:

King William had a castle in Normandy, at a place called L'Aigle. He was spending some time there, in the year 1076, with his court and family. One day William Rufus and Henry were in one of the upper apartments of the castle, playing with dice, and amusing themselves, in company with other young men of the court, in various ways. There was a window in the apartment leading out upon a balcony, from which one might look down upon the courtyard of the castle below. Robert was in this courtyard with some of *his* companions, walking there in an irritated state of mind, which had been produced by some previous disputes with his brothers. William Rufus looked down from the balcony and saw him, and by way, perhaps, of quenching his anger, poured some water down upon him. The deed changed the suppressed and silent irritation in Robert's heart to a perfect phrensy of rage and revenge. He drew his sword and sprang to the staircase. He uttered loud and terrible imprecations as he went, declaring that he would kill the author of such an insult, even if he *was* his brother. The courtyard was, of course, immediately filled with shouts and exclamations of alarm, and everybody pressed forward toward the room from which the water had been thrown, some to witness, and some to prevent the affray.

The king himself, who happened to be in that part of the castle at the time, was one of the number. He reached the apartment just in time to interpose between his sons, and prevent the commission of the awful crime of fratricide. As it was, he found it extremely difficult to part the ferocious combatants. It required all his paternal authority, and not a little actual force, to arrest the affray. He succeeded, however, at length, with the help of the by-standers, in parting his sons, and Robert, out of breath, and pale with impotent rage, was led away.

Robert considered his father as taking sides against him in this quarrel, and he declared that he could not, and would not, endure such treatment any longer. He found some sympathy in the conversation of his mother, to whom he went immediately with bitter complainings. She tried to soothe and quiet his wounded spirit, but he would not be pacified. He spent the afternoon and evening in organizing a party of wild and desperate young men from among the nobles of the court, with a view of raising a rebellion against his father, and getting possession of Normandy by force. They kept their designs profoundly secret, but prepared to leave L'Aigle that night, to go and seize Rouen, the capital, which they hoped to surprise into a surrender. Accordingly, in the middle of the night, the desperate troop mounted their horses and rode away. In the morning the king found that they were gone, and he sent an armed force after them. Their plan of surprising Rouen failed. The king's detachment overtook them, and, after a sharp contest, succeeded in capturing a few of the rebels, though Robert himself, accompanied by some of the more desperate of his followers, escaped over the frontier into a neighboring province, where he sought refuge in the castle of one of his father's enemies.

This result, as might have been expected, filled the mind of Matilda with anxiety and distress. A civil war between her husband and her son was now inevitable; and while every consideration of prudence and of duty required her to espouse the father's cause, her maternal love, a principle stronger far, in most cases, than prudence and duty combined, drew her irresistibly toward her son. Robert collected around him all the discontented and desperate spirits of the realm, and for a long time continued to make his father infinite trouble. Matilda, while she forbore to advocate his cause openly in the presence of the king, kept up a secret communication with him. She sent him information and advice from time to time, and sometimes supplies, and was thus, technically, guilty of a great crime—the crime of maintaining a treasonable correspondence with a rebel. In a moral point of view, however, her conduct may have been entirely right; at any rate, its influence was very salutary, for she did all in her power to restrain both the father and the son; and by the influence which she thus exerted, she doubtless mitigated very much the fierceness of the struggle.

Of course, the advantage, in such a civil war as this, would be wholly on the side of the sovereign. William had all the power and resources of the kingdom in his own hands—the army, the towns, the castles, the treasures. Robert had a troop of wild, desperate, and unmanageable outlaws, without authority, without money, without a sense of justice on their side. He gradually became satisfied that the contest was vain. In proportion as the activity of the hostilities diminished, Matilda became more and more open in her efforts to restrain it, and to allay the animosity on either side. She succeeded, finally, in inducing Robert to lay down his arms, and then brought about an interview between the parties, in hopes of a peaceful settlement of the quarrel.

It appeared very soon, however, at this interview, that there was no hope of anything like a real and cordial reconciliation. Though both the father and son had become weary of the unnatural war which they had waged against each other, yet the ambitious and selfish desires on both sides, in which the contest had originated, remained unchanged. Robert began the conference by imperiously demanding of his father the fulfillment of his promise to give him the government of Normandy. His father replied by reproaching him with his unnatural and wicked rebellion, and warned him of the danger he incurred, in imitating the example of Absalom, of sharing that wretched rebel's fate. Robert rejoined that he did not come to meet his father for the sake of hearing a sermon preached. He had had enough of sermons, he said, when he was a boy, studying grammar. He wanted his father to do him justice, not preach to him. The king said that he should never divide his dominions, while he lived, with anyone; and added, notwithstanding what Robert had contemptuously said about sermons, that the Scripture declared that a house divided against itself could not stand. He then proceeded to reproach and incriminate the prince in the severest manner for his disloyalty as a subject, and his undutifulness and ingratitude as a son. It was intolerable, he said, that a son should become the rival and bitterest enemy of his father, when it was to him that he owed, not merely all that he enjoyed, but his very existence itself.

These reproaches were probably uttered in an imperious and angry manner, and with that spirit of denunciation which only irritates the accused and arouses his resentment, instead of awakening feelings of penitence and contrition. At any rate, the thought of his filial ingratitude, as his father presented it, produced no relenting in Robert's mind. He abruptly terminated the interview, and went out of his father's presence in a rage.

In spite of all his mother's exertions and entreaties, he resolved to leave the country once more. He said he would rather be an exile, and wander homeless in foreign lands, than to remain in his father's court, and be treated in so unjust and ignominious a manner, by one who was bound by the strongest possible obligations to be his best and truest friend. Matilda could not induce him to change this determination; and, accordingly, taking with him a few of the most desperate and dissolute of his companions, he went northward, crossed the frontier, and sought refuge in Flanders. Flanders, it will be recollected, was Matilda's native land. Her brother was the Earl of Flanders at this time. The earl received young Robert very cordially, both for his sister's sake, and also, probably, in some degree, as a means of petty hostility against King William, his powerful neighbor, whose glory and good fortune he envied.

Robert had not the means or the resources necessary for renewing an open war with his father, but his disposition to do this was as strong as ever, and he began immediately to open secret communications and correspondence with all the nobles and barons in Normandy whom he thought disposed to espouse his cause. He succeeded in inducing them to make secret contributions of funds to supply his pecuniary wants, of course promising to repay them with ample grants and rewards so soon as he should obtain his rights. He maintained similar communications, too, with Matilda, though she kept them very profoundly secret from her husband.

Robert had other friends besides those whom he found thus furtively in Normandy. The King of France himself was much pleased at the breaking out of this terrible feud in the family of his neighbor, who, from being his dependent and vassal, had become, by his conquest of England, his great competitor and rival in the estimation of mankind. Philip was disposed to rejoice at any occurrences which tended to tarnish William's glory, or which threatened a division and diminution of his power. He directed his agents, therefore, both in Normandy and in Flanders, to encourage and promote the dissension by every means in their power. He took great care not to commit himself by any open and positive promises of aid, and yet still he contrived, by a thousand indirect means, to encourage Robert to expect it. Thus the mischief was widened and extended, while yet nothing effectual was done toward organizing an insurrection. In fact, Robert had neither the means nor the mental capacity necessary for maturing and carrying into effect any actual plan of rebellion. In the meantime, months passed away, and as nothing effectual was done, Robert's adherents in Normandy became gradually discouraged. They ceased their contributions, and gradually forgot their absent and incompetent leader. Robert spent his time in dissipation and vice, squandering in feasts and in the company of abandoned men and women the means which his followers sent him to enable him to prepare for the war; and when, at last, these supplies failed him, he would have been reduced gradually to great distress and destitution, were it not that one faithful and devoted friend still adhered to him. That friend was his mother.

Matilda knew very well that whatever she did for her absent son must be done in the most clandestine manner, and this required much stratagem and contrivance on her part. She was aided, however, in her efforts at concealment by her husband's absence. He was now for a time in England, having been called there by some pressing demands of public duty. He left a great minister of state in charge of Normandy, whose vigilance Matilda thought it would be comparatively easy to elude. She sent to Robert, in Flanders, first her own private funds. Then she employed for this purpose a portion of such public funds as came into her hands. The more she sent, however, the more frequent and imperious were Robert's demands for fresh supplies. The resources of a mother, whether great or small, are always soon exhausted by the insatiable requirements of a dissolute and profligate son. When Matilda's money was gone, she sold her jewels, then her more expensive clothes, and, finally, such objects of value, belonging to herself or to her husband, as could be most easily and privately disposed of. The minister, who was very faithful and watchful in the discharge of his duties, observed indications that something mysterious was going on. His suspicions were aroused. He watched Matilda's movements, and soon discovered the truth. He sent information to William. William could not believe it possible that his minister's surmises could be true; for William was simply a statesman and a soldier, and had very inadequate ideas of the absorbing and uncontrollable power which is exercised by the principle of maternal love.

He, however, determined immediately to take most efficient measures to ascertain the truth. He returned to Normandy, and there he succeeded in intercepting one of Matilda's messengers on his way to Flanders, with communications and money for Robert. The name of this messenger was Sampson. William seized the money and the letters, and sent the messenger to one of his castles, to be shut up in a dungeon. Then, with the proofs of guilt which he had thus obtained, he went, full of astonishment and anger, to find Matilda, and to upbraid her, as he thought she deserved, for her base and ungrateful betrayal of her husband.

The reproaches which he addressed to her were bitter and stern, though they seem to have been spoken in a tone of sorrow rather than of anger. "I am sure," he said, "I have ever been to you a faithful and devoted husband. I do not know what more you could have desired than I have done. I have loved you with a sincere and true affection. I have honored you. I have placed you in the highest positions, intrusting you repeatedly with large shares of my own sovereign power. I have confided in you—committing my most essential and vital interests to your charge. And now this is the return. You employ the very position, and power, and means which your confiding husband has put into your hands, to betray him in the most cruel way, and to aid and encourage his worst and most dangerous enemy."

To these reproaches Matilda attempted no reply, except to plead the irresistible impetuosity and strength of her maternal love. "I could not bear," she said, "to leave Robert in distress and suffering while I had any possible means of relieving him. He is my child. I think of him all the time. I love him more than my life. I solemnly declare to you, that if he were now dead, and I could restore him to life by dying for him, I would most gladly do it. How, then, do you suppose that I could possibly live here in abundance and luxury, while he was wandering homeless, in destitution and want, and not try to relieve him? Whether it is right or wrong for me to feel so, I do not know; but this I know, I *must* feel so: I cannot help it. He is our first-born son; I cannot abandon him."

William went away from the presence of Matilda full of resentment and anger. Of course, he could do nothing in respect to her but reproach her, but he determined that the unlucky Sampson should suffer severely for the crime. He sent orders to the castle where he lay immured, requiring that his eyes should be put out. Matilda, however, discovered the danger which threatened her messenger in time to send him warning. He contrived to make his escape, and fled to a certain monastery which was under Matilda's special patronage and charge. A monastery was, in those days, a sanctuary into which the arm even of the most despotic authority scarcely dared to intrude in pursuit of its victim. To make the safety doubly sure, the abbot proposed that the trembling fugitive should join their order and become a monk. Sampson was willing to do anything to save his life. The operation of putting out the eyes was very generally fatal, so that he considered his life at stake. He was, accordingly, shaven and shorn, and clothed in the monastic garb. He assumed the vows of the order, and entered, with his brother monks, upon the course of fastings, penances, and prayers which pertained to his new vocation; and William left him to pursue it in peace.

Things went on worse instead of better after this discovery of the mother's participation in the councils of the son. Either through the aid which his mother had rendered, or by other means, there seemed to be a strong party in and out of Normandy who were inclined to espouse Robert's cause. His friends, at length, raised a very considerable army, and putting him at the head of it, they advanced to attack Rouen. The king, greatly alarmed at this danger, collected all the forces that he could command, and went to meet his rebel son. William Rufus accompanied his father, intending to fight by his side; while Matilda, in an agony of terror and distress, remained, half distracted, within her castle walls—as a wife and mother might be expected to be, on the approach of a murderous conflict between her husband and her son. The thought that one of them might, perhaps, be actually killed by the other, filled her with dismay.

And, in fact, this dreadful result came very near being realized. Robert, in the castle at L'Aigle, had barely been prevented from destroying his brother, and now, on the plain of Archembraye, where this battle was fought, his father *fell*, and was very near being killed, by his hand. In the midst of the fight, while the horsemen were impetuously charging each other in various parts of the field, all so disguised by their armor that no one could know the individual with whom he was contending, Robert encountered a large and powerful knight, and drove his lance through his armor into his arm. Through the shock of the encounter and the faintness produced by the agony of the wound, the horseman fell to the ground, and Robert perceived, by the voice with which his fallen enemy cried out in his pain and terror, that it was his father that he had thus pierced with his steel. At the same moment, the wounded father, in looking at his victorious antagonist, recognized his son. He cursed his unnatural enemy with a bitter and terrible malediction. Robert was shocked and terrified at what he had done. He leaped from his horse, knelt down by the side of his father, and called for aid. The king, distracted by the anguish of his wound, and by the burning indignation and resentment which raged in his bosom against the unnatural hostility which inflicted it, turned away from his son, and refused to receive any succor from him.

Besides the misfortune of being unhorsed and wounded, the battle itself went that day against the king. Robert's army remained masters of the field. William Rufus was wounded too, as well as his father. Matilda was overwhelmed with distress and mental anguish at the result. She could not endure the idea of allowing so unnatural and dreadful a struggle to go on. She begged her husband, with the most earnest importunities and with many tears, to find some way of accommodating the dispute. Her nights were sleepless, her days were spent in weeping, and her health and strength were soon found to be wasting very rapidly away. She was emaciated, wan, and pale, and it was plain that such distress, if long continued, would soon bring her to the grave.

Matilda's intercessions at length prevailed. The king sent for his son, and, after various negotiations, some sort of compromise was effected. The armies were disbanded, peace was restored, and Robert and his father once more seemed to be friends. Soon after this, William, having a campaign to make in the north of England, took Robert with him as one of the generals in his army.

12

The Conclusion

A.D. 1078-1087

William's reign in England.—His difficulties.—Feelings of the English people.—Rebellions.—Amalgamation of the English and Normans.—William's labors.—Necessity of bringing a large Norman force.—Providing for them.—The British realm Normanized.—O yes! O yes! O yes!—Relics of the past.—Their future preservation.—Point of view in which the Norman Conquest is regarded.—Domesday Book.—Its great obscurity.—Specimen of the Domesday Book.—Translation.—Matilda's health declines.—Death of her daughter.—Matilda retires to her palace at Caen.—Her distress of mind.—Matilda's health.—Memorials of her.—William's declining years.—His fitfulness and discontent.—Philip ridicules William.—William's rage.—William's threats.—Conflagration of Mantes.—William's injury.—His great danger.—William's remorse.—His last acts.—Robert absent.—He receives Normandy.—William Rufus and Henry.—The king's will.—William's death.—Abandonment of the body.—Apprehensions of the people.—The body removed to Caen.—Extraordinary scenes.—The body conveyed to the monastery on a cart.—The procession broken up.—Scene at the interment.—The sarcophagus too small.—The body burst.—William Rufus obtains possession of the English throne.

WILLIAM THE CONQUEROR

FROM the time of the battle of Hastings, which took place in 1066, to that of William's death, which occurred in 1087, there intervened a period of about twenty years, during which the great monarch reigned over his extended dominions with a very despotic sway, though not without a large share of the usual dangers, difficulties, and struggles attending such a rule. He brought over immense numbers of Normans from Normandy into England, and placed all the military and civil power of the empire in their hands; and he relied almost entirely upon the superiority of his physical force for keeping the country in subjugation to his sway. It is true, he maintained that he was the rightful heir to the English crown, and that, consequently, the tenure by which he held it was the right of inheritance, and not the right of conquest; and he professed to believe that the people of England generally admitted his claim. This was, in fact, to a considerable extent, true. At least there was probably a large part of the population who believed William's right to the crown superior to that of Harold, whom he had deposed. Still, as William was by birth, and education, and language a foreigner, and as all the friends and followers who attended him, and, in fact, almost the whole of the army, on which he mainly relied for the preservation of his power, were foreigners too—wearing a strange dress, and speaking in an unknown tongue—the great mass of the English people could not but feel that they were under a species of foreign subjugation. Quarrels were therefore continually breaking out between them and their Norman masters, resulting in fierce and bloody struggles, on their part, to get free. These rebellions were always effectually put down; but when quelled in one quarter they soon broke out in another, and they kept William and his forces almost always employed.

But William was not a mere warrior. He was well aware that the permanence and stability of his own and his successor's sway in England would depend finally upon the kind of basis on which the civil institutions of the country should rest, and on the proper consolidation and adjustment of the administrative and judicial functions of the realm. In the intervals of his campaigns, therefore, William devoted a great deal of time and attention to this subject, and he evinced a most profound and statesmanlike wisdom and sagacity in his manner of treating it.

He had, in fact, a Herculean task to perform—a double task—viz., to amalgamate two *nations*, and also to fuse and merge two *languages* into one. He was absolutely compelled, by the circumstances under which he was placed, to grapple with both these vast undertakings. If, at the time when, in his park at Rouen, he first heard of Harold's accession, he had supposed that there was a party in England in his favor strong enough to allow of his proceeding there alone, or with a small Norman attendance, so that he might rely mainly on the English themselves for his accession to the throne, the formidable difficulties which, as it was, he had subsequently to encounter, would all have been saved. But there was no such party—at least there was no evidence that there was one of sufficient strength to justify him in trusting himself to it. It seemed to him, then, that if he undertook to gain possession of the English throne at all, he must rely entirely on the force which he could take with him from Normandy. To make this reliance effectual, the force so taken must be an overwhelming one. Then, if Normans in great numbers were to go to England for the purpose of putting him upon the English throne, they must be rewarded, and so vast a number of candidates for the prizes of honor and wealth could be satisfied only in England, and by confiscations there. His possessions in Normandy would obviously be insufficient for such a purpose. It was evident, moreover, that if a large number of Norman adventurers were placed in stations of trust and honor, and charged with civil offices and administrative functions all over England, they would form a sort of class by themselves, and would be looked upon with jealousy and envy by the original inhabitants, and that there was no hope of maintaining them safely in their position except by making the class as numerous and as strong as possible. In a word, William saw very clearly that, while it would have been very well, if it had been possible, for him to have brought *no* Normans to England, it was clearly best, since so many must go, to contrive every means to swell and increase the number. It was one of those cases where, being obliged to go far, it is best to go farther; and William resolved on thoroughly *Normanizing*, so to speak, the whole British realm. This enormous undertaking he accomplished fully and permanently; and the institutions of England, the lines of family descent, the routine of judicial and administrative business, and the very language of the realm, retain the Norman characteristics which he ingrafted into them to the present day.

It gives us a feeling akin to that of sublimity to find, even in our own land, and in the most remote situations of it, the lingering relics of the revolutions and deeds of these early ages, still remaining, like a faint ripple rolling gently upon a beach in a deep and secluded bay, which was set in motion, perhaps, at first, as one of the mountainous surges of a wintery storm in the most distant seas. For example, if we enter the most humble court in any remote and newly-settled country in the American forests, a plain and rustic-looking man will call the equally rustic-looking assembly to order by rapping his baton, the only symbol of his office, on the floor, and calling out, in words mystic and meaningless to him, "O yes! O yes! O yes!" [Oyez! Oyez! Oyez! Norman French for Hearken! hearken! hearken!] He little thinks that he is obeying a behest of William the Conqueror, issued eight hundred years ago, ordaining that his native tongue should be employed in the courts of England. The irresistible progress of improvement and reform have gradually displaced the intruding language again—except so far as it has become merged and incorporated with the common language of the country—from all the ordinary forms of legal proceedings. It lingers still, however, as it were, on the threshold, in this call to order; and as it is harmless there, the spirit of conservatism will, perhaps, preserve for it this last place of refuge for a thousand years to come, and *"O yes"* will be the phrase for ordaining silence by many generations of officers, who will, perhaps, never have heard of the authority whose orders they unwittingly obey.

The work of incorporating the Norman and English families with one another, and fusing the two languages into one, required about a century for its full accomplishment; and when at last it was accomplished, the people of England were somewhat puzzled to know whether they ought to feel proud of William's exploits in the conquest of England, or humiliated by them. So far as they were themselves descended from the Normans, the conquest was one of the glorious deeds of their ancestors. So far as they were of English parentage, it would seem to be incumbent on them to mourn over their fathers' defeat. It is obvious that from such a species of perplexity as this there was no escape, and it has accordingly continued to embarrass the successive generations of Englishmen down to the present day. The Norman Conquest occupies, therefore, a very uncertain and equivocal position in English history, the various modern writers who look back to it now being hardly able to determine whether they are to regard it as a mortifying subjugation which their ancestors suffered, or a glorious victory which they gained.

One of the great measures of William's reign, and one, in fact, for which it has been particularly famous in modern times, was a grand census or registration of the kingdom, which the Conqueror ordered with a view of having on record a perfect enumeration and description of all the real and personal property in the kingdom. This grand national survey was made in 1078. The result was recorded in two volumes of different sizes, which were called the Great and the Little Domesday Book. These books are still preserved, and are to this day of the very highest authority in respect to all questions touching ancient rights of property. One is a folio, and the other a quarto volume. The records are written on vellum, in a close, abridged, and, to ordinary readers, a perfectly unintelligible character. The language is Latin; but a modern Latin scholar, without any means other than an inspection of the work, would be utterly unable to decipher it. In fact, though the character is highly wrought, and in some respects elegant, the whole style and arrangement of the work is pretty nearly on a par, in respect to scientific skill, with Queen Emma's designs upon the Bayeux tapestry. About half a century ago, copies of these works were printed, by means of type made to represent the original character. But these printed editions were found unintelligible and useless until copious indexes were prepared, and published to accompany them, at great expense of time and labor.

Some little idea of the character and style of this celebrated record may be obtained from the following specimen, which is as faithful an imitation of the original as any ordinary typography will allow:

> In Brixistan Hund'.
> Rex ten Bermundesye. heraldº tenuit. Tc se det'd
> p. xiii. hid. m° p. xii. hid. Tra. e. viii. car. In dnio. e una
> car. 7 xxv. villi 7 xxxiii. bord cu. un. car.
> Ibi nova 7 pulchra eccla. 7 xx. ac p ti. Silvaf v. porc
> de pasnag:

Excerpt from the Domesday Book

The passage, deciphered and expressed in full, stands thus—the letters omitted in the original, above, being supplied in italics:

IN BRIXISTAN HUND*redo*.

Rex ten*et* BERMUNDESYE. HERALD*US* com*es*tenuit. T*unc* se def*end*ebat pro xiii. hid*is*, m*od*o pro xii. hid*is*. T*er*ra est viii. car*ruc*atarum. In dom*i*nio est una car*r*ucata et xxv. vill*ani* et xxxiii. bord*arii* cu*m* un*a* car*ruc*ata. Ibi nova et pulchra eccl*esia*, et xx. acr*æ* pr*a*ti. Silva v. porc*is* de pasnag*io*.

The English translation is as follows:

IN BRIXISTAN HUNDRED.

The king holds BERMUNDESYE. Earl HERALD held it [before]. At that time it was rated at thirteen hides; now, at twelve. The arable land is eight carrucates [*or* plow-lands]. There is one carrucate in demesne, and twenty-five villans, and thirty-three bordars, with one carrucate. There is a new and handsome church, with twenty acres of meadow, and woodland for five hogs in pasnage [pasturage] time.

But we must pass on to the conclusion of the story. About the year 1082, Queen Matilda's health began seriously to decline. She was harassed by a great many anxieties and cares connected with the affairs of state which devolved upon her, and arising from the situation of her family: these anxieties produced great dejection of spirits, and aggravated, if they did not wholly cause, her bodily disease. She was at this time in Normandy. One great source of her mental suffering was her anxiety in respect to one of her daughters, who, as well as herself, was declining in health. Forgetting her own danger in her earnest desires for the welfare of her child, she made a sort of pilgrimage to a monastery which contained the shrine of a certain saint, who, as she imagined, had power to save her daughter. She laid a rich present on the shrine; she offered before it most earnest prayers, imploring, with tears of bitter grief, the intercession of the saint, and manifesting every outward symbol of humility and faith. She took her place in the religious services of the monastery, and conformed to its usages, as if she had been in the humblest private station. But all was in vain. The health of her beloved daughter continued to fail, until at length she died; and Matilda, growing herself more feeble, and almost broken hearted through grief, shut herself up in the palace at Caen.

It was in the same palace which William had built, within his monastery, many long years before, at the time of their marriage. Matilda looked back to that period, and to the buoyant hopes and bright anticipations of power, glory, and happiness which then filled her heart, with sadness and sorrow. The power and the glory had been attained, and in a measure tenfold greater than she had imagined, but the happiness had never come. Ambition had been contending unceasingly for twenty years, among all the branches of her family, against domestic peace and love. She possessed, herself, an aspiring mind, but the principles of maternal and conjugal love were stronger in her heart than those of ambition; and yet she was compelled to see ambition bearing down and destroying love in all its forms every where around her. Her last days were embittered by the breaking out of new contests between her husband and her son.

Matilda sought for peace and comfort in multiplying her religious services and observances. She fasted, she prayed, she interceded for the forgiveness of her sins with many tears. The monks celebrated mass at her bed-side, and made, as she thought, by renewing the sacrifice of Christ, a fresh propitiation for her sins. William, who was then in Normandy, hearing of her forlorn and unhappy condition, came to see her. He arrived just in time to see her die.

They conveyed her body from the palace in her husband's monastery at Caen to the convent which she had built. It was received there in solemn state, and deposited in the tomb. For centuries afterward, there remained many memorials of her existence and her greatness there, in paintings, embroideries, sacred gifts, and records, which have been gradually wasted away by the hand of time. They have not, however, wholly disappeared, for travelers who visit the spot find that many memorials and traditions of Matilda linger there still.

William himself did not live many years after the death of his wife. He was several years older than she. In fact, he was now considerably advanced in age. He became extremely corpulent as he grew old, which, as he was originally of a large frame, made him excessively unwieldy. The inconvenience resulting from this habit of body was not the only evil that attended it. It affected his health, and even threatened to end in serious if not fatal disease. While he was thus made comparatively helpless in body by the infirmities of his advancing age, he was nevertheless as active and restless in spirit as ever. It was, however, no longer the activity of youth, and hope, and progress which animated him, but rather the fitful uneasiness with which age agitates itself under the vexations which it sometimes has to endure, or struggles convulsively at the approach of real or imaginary dangers, threatening the possessions which it has been the work of life to gain. The dangers in William's case were real, not imaginary. He was continually threatened on every side. In fact, the very year before he died, the dissensions between himself and Robert broke out anew, and he was obliged, unwieldy and helpless as he was, to repair to Normandy, at the head of an armed force, to quell the disturbances which Robert and his partisans had raised.

Robert was countenanced and aided at this time by Philip, the king of France, who had always been King William's jealous and implacable rival. Philip, who, as will be recollected, was very young when William asked his aid at the time of his invasion of England, was now in middle life, and at the height of his power. As he had refused William his aid, he was naturally somewhat envious and jealous of his success, and he was always ready to take part against him. He now aided and abetted Robert in his turbulence and insubordination, and ridiculed the helpless infirmities of the aged king.

While William was in Normandy, he submitted to a course of medical treatment, in the hope of diminishing his excessive corpulency, and relieving the disagreeable and dangerous symptoms which attended it. While thus in his physician's hands, he was, of course, confined to his chamber. Philip, in ridicule, called it "being in the straw." He asked some one who appeared at his court, having recently arrived from Normandy, whether the old woman of England was still in the straw. Some miserable tale-bearer, such as every where infest society at the present day, who delight in quoting to one friend what they think will excite their anger against another, repeated these words to William. Sick as he was, the sarcasm aroused him to a furious paroxysm of rage. He swore by "God's brightness and resurrection" that, when he got out again, he would kindle such fires in Philip's dominions, in commemoration of his delivery, as should make his realms too hot to hold him.

He kept his word—at least so far as respects the kindling of the fires; but the fires, instead of making Philip's realms too hot to hold him, by a strange yet just retribution, were simply the means of closing forever the mortal career of the hand that kindled them. The circumstances of this final scene of the great conqueror's earthly history were these:

In the execution of his threat to make Philip's dominions too hot to hold him, William, as soon as he was able to mount his horse, headed an expedition, and crossed the frontiers of Normandy, and moved forward into the heart of France, laying waste the country, as he advanced, with fire and sword. He came soon to the town of Mantes, a town upon the Seine, directly on the road to Paris. William's soldiers attacked the town with furious impetuosity, carried it by assault, and set it on fire. William followed them in, through the gates, glorying in the fulfillment of his threats of vengeance. Some timbers from a burning house had fallen into the street, and, burning there, had left a smoldering bed of embers, in which the fire was still remaining. William, excited with the feeling of exultation and victory, was riding unguardedly on through the scene of ruin he had made, issuing orders, and shouting in a frantic manner as he went, when he was suddenly stopped by a violent recoil of his horse from the burning embers, on which he had stepped, and which had been concealed from view by the ashes which covered them. William, unwieldy and comparatively helpless as he was, was thrown with great force upon the pommel of the saddle. He saved himself from falling from the horse, but he immediately found that he had sustained some serious internal injury. He was obliged to dismount, and to be conveyed away, by a very sudden transition, from the dreadful scene of conflagration and vengeance which he had been enacting, to the solemn chamber of death. They made a litter for him, and a corps of strong men was designated to bear the heavy and now helpless burden back to Normandy.

They took the suffering monarch to Rouen. The ablest physicians were summoned to his bed-side. After examining his case, they concluded that he must die. The tidings threw the unhappy patient into a state of extreme anxiety and terror. The recollection of the thousand deeds of selfish ambition and cruelty which he had been perpetrating, he said, all his days, filled him with remorse. He shrunk back with invincible dread from the hour, now so rapidly approaching, when he was to appear in judgment before God, and answer, like any common mortal, for his crimes. He had been accustomed all his life to consider himself as above all law, superior to all power, and beyond the reach of all judicial question. But now his time had come. He who had so often made others tremble, trembled now in his turn, with an acuteness of terror and distress which only the boldest and most high-handed offenders ever feel. He cried bitterly to God for forgiveness, and brought the monks around him to help him with incessant prayers. He ordered all the money that he had on hand to be given to the poor. He sent commands to have the churches which he had burned at Mantes rebuilt, and the other injuries which he had effected in his anger repaired. In a word, he gave himself very earnestly to the work of attempting, by all the means considered most efficacious in those days, to avert and appease the dreaded anger of heaven.

William's Horse Stepping Upon the Embers

Of his three oldest sons, Robert was away; the quarrel between him and his father had become irreconcilable, and he would not come to visit him, even in his dying hours. William Rufus and Henry were there, and they remained very constantly at their father's bed-side—not, however, from a principle of filial affection, but because they wanted to be present when he should express his last wishes in respect to the disposal of his dominions. Such an expression, though oral, would be binding as a will. When, at length, the king gave his dying directions in respect to the succession, it appeared that, after all, he considered his right to the English throne as very doubtful in the sight of God. He had, in a former part of his life, promised Normandy to Robert, as his inheritance, when he himself should die; and though he had so often refused to surrender it to him while he himself continued to live, he confirmed his title to the succession now. "I have promised it to him," he said, "and I keep my promise; and yet I know that that will be a miserable country which is subject to his government. He is a proud and foolish knave, and can never prosper. As for my kingdom of England," he continued, "I bequeath it to no one, for it was not bequeathed to me. I acquired it by force, and at the price of blood. I leave it in the hands of God, only wishing that my son William Rufus may have it, for he has been submissive to me in all things." "And what do you give *me*, father?" asked Henry, eagerly, at this point. "I give you," said the king, "five thousand pounds from my treasury." "But what shall I do with my five thousand pounds," asked Henry, "if you do not give me either house or land?" "Be quiet, my son," rejoined the king, "and trust in God. Let your brothers go before you; your turn will come after theirs."

The object which had kept the young men at their father's bed-side having been now attained, they both withdrew. Henry went to get his money, and William Rufus set off immediately for England, to prepare the way for his own accession to the throne, as soon as his father should be no more.

The king determined to be removed from his castle in Rouen to a monastery which was situated at a short distance from the city, without the walls. The noise of the city disturbed him, and, besides, he thought he should feel safer to die on sacred ground. He was accordingly removed to the monastery. There, on the tenth of September, he was awakened in the morning by hearing the city bells ringing. He asked what it meant. He was told that the bells were ringing for the morning service at the church of St. Mary. He lifted up his hands, looked to heaven, and said, "I commend myself to my Lady Mary, the holy Mother of God," and almost immediately expired.

The readers of history have frequent occasion to be surprised at the sudden and total change which often takes place at the moment of the death of a mighty sovereign, and even sometimes before his death, in the indications of the respect and consideration with which his attendants and followers regard him. In William's case, as has happened in many other cases since, the moment he ceased to breathe he was utterly abandoned. Every body fled, carrying with them, as they went, whatever they could seize from the chamber—the arms, the furniture, the dresses, and the plate; for all these articles became their perquisites on the decease of their master. The almost incredible statement is made that the heartless monsters actually stripped the dead body of their sovereign, to make sure of all their dues, and left it naked on the stone floor, while they bore their prizes to a place of safety. The body lay in this neglected state for many hours; for the tidings of the great monarch's death, which was so sudden at last, produced, as it spread, universal excitement and apprehension. No one knew to what changes the event would lead, what wars would follow between the sons, or what insurrections or rebellions might have been secretly formed, to break out suddenly when this crisis should have arrived. Thus the whole community were thrown into a state of excitement and confusion.

The monk and lay brethren of the monastery at length came in, took up the body, and prepared it for burial. They then brought crosses, tapers, and censers, and began to offer prayers and to chant requiems for the repose of the soul of the deceased. They sent also the Archbishop of Rouen, to know what was to be done with the body. The archbishop gave orders that it should be taken to Caen, and be deposited there in the monastery which William had erected at the time of his marriage.

The tale which the ancient historians have told in respect to the interment is still more extraordinary, and more inconsistent with all the ideas we naturally form of the kind of consideration and honor which the remains of so great a potentate would receive at the hands of his household and his officers of state, than the account of his death. It is said that all the members of his household, and all his officers, immediately after his decease, abandoned the town—all eagerly occupied in plans and maneuvers to secure their positions under the new reign. Some went in pursuit of Robert, and some to follow William Rufus. Henry locked up his money in a strong box, well ironed, and went off with it to find some place of security. There was nobody left to take the neglected body to the grave.

At last a countryman was found who undertook to transport the heavy burden from Rouen to Caen. He procured a cart, and conveyed it from the monastery to the river, where it was put on board a vessel, and taken down the Seine to its mouth, and thence by sea to Caen. The Abbot of St. Stephen's, which was the name of William's monastery there, came, with some monks and a procession of the people, to accompany the body to the abbey. As this procession was moving along, however, a fire broke out in the town, and the attendants, actuated either by a sense of duty requiring them to aid in extinguishing the flames, or by curiosity to witness the conflagration, abandoned the funeral cortège. The procession was broken up, and the whole multitude, clergy and laity, went off to the fire, leaving the coffin, with its bearers, alone. The bearers, however, went on, and conveyed their charge to the church within the abbey walls.

When the time arrived for the interment, a great company assembled to witness the ceremonies. Stones had been taken up in the church floor, and a grave dug. A stone coffin, a sort of sarcophagus, had been prepared, and placed in the grave as a receptacle for the body. When all was ready, and the body was about to be let down, a man suddenly came forward from the crowd and arrested the proceedings. He said that the land on which the abbey stood belonged to him; that William had taken forcible possession of it, for the abbey, at the time of his marriage; that he, the owner, had been compelled thus far to submit to this wrong, inasmuch as he had, during William's life-time, no means of redress, but now he protested against a spoliation. "The land," he said, "is mine; it belonged to my father. I have not sold it, or forfeited it, nor pledged it, nor given it. It is my right. I claim it. In the name of God, I forbid you to put the body of the spoiler there, or to cover him with my ground."

When the excitement and surprise which this denunciation had awakened had subsided a little, the bishops called this sudden claimant aside, examined the proofs of his allegations, and, finding that the case was truly as he stated it, they paid him, on the spot, a sum equal to the value of ground enough for a grave, and promised to take immediate measures for the payment of the rest. The remonstrant then consented that the interment might proceed.

In attempting to let the body down into the place prepared for it, they found that the sarcophagus was too small. They undertook to force the body in. In attempting this, the coffin was broken, and the body, already, through the long delays, advanced in decomposition, was burst. The monks brought incense and perfumes, and burned and sprinkled them around the place, but in vain. The church was so offensive that everybody abandoned it at once, except the workmen who remained to fill the grave.

* * *

While these things were transpiring in Normandy, William Rufus had hastened to England, taking with him the evidences of his father's dying wish that he should succeed him on the English throne. Before he reached headquarters there, he heard of his father's death, and he succeeded in inducing the Norman chieftains to proclaim him king. Robert's friends made an effort to advance his claims, but they could do nothing effectual for him, and so it was soon settled, by a treaty between the brothers, that William Rufus should reign in England, while Robert was to content himself with his father's ancient domain of Normandy.

THE END

ABOUT JACOB ABBOTT

Early Life and Education

Jacob Abbott was born in Hallowell, Maine in 1803, the son of a minister and farmer. Even as a young boy, he showed academic promise and an interest in spiritual matters. After attending the Hallowell Academy, he was admitted to Bowdoin College at the age of 14.

At Bowdoin, Abbott studied classics and mathematics. He graduated second in his class in 1820 at the young age of 16. He was known as a serious and studious young man who strove for excellence.

After college, Abbott went on to study at Andover Theological Seminary with the intention of becoming a Congregationalist minister. However, his rigorous study habits and frail health caused him to abandon this pursuit after just two years.

Health Issues and Early Career

Abbott was plagued by gastrointestinal issues and migraines throughout his life, likely exacerbated by the demanding academic environment. His poor health finally forced him to leave his ministerial studies and turn to the less stressful pursuits of writing and tutoring.

First, Abbott took a job as a professor of mathematics and natural philosophy at Amherst College in 1824. The following year, he married Harriet Vaughan and moved to Boston where he opened a school for

ABOUT JACOB ABBOTT

young ladies. It was during this time that he began writing simple textbooks for teaching science, history and Christian values.

So while Abbott had aspired to be a minister, chronic health issues led him to find an alternate calling educating children through clear and engaging writing. This pivot would launch his successful career as one of the most famous children's authors of the 19th century.

In 1825, Abbott married Harriet Vaughan and soon after started his own school for young ladies in Boston. During this time, he began writing educational books in a popular, simple style. His early works included the Mount Vernon Reader and The Young Christian.

Abbott gained fame with the Rollo series, first published in 1835. These stories followed a young boy named Rollo learning morals and virtues through his everyday adventures. The series was hugely popular and established Abbott's reputation as a gifted children's writer.

Other notable books by Abbott include the Franconia Stories (1853-1873), a 10-volume series about a brother and sister's adventures in the country, and the Marco Paul series (1853-1873), which followed a boy's travels around America learning about each state.

In all, Jacob Abbott wrote over 200 books, primarily for young readers. His works were praised for their ability to educate and impart moral lessons in an engaging, story-driven way. Though largely forgotten today, he was one of the most prolific and beloved children's authors of his era.

A number of the books Abbott wrote were biographies of famous people. Famous characters covered in these books included:

Alexander the Great: This book provides a sweeping look at the life and achievements of Alexander III of Macedon, better known as Alexander the Great. It follows his early education by Aristotle, ascension to the throne after his father Philip II's assassination, and extensive military campaigns across Asia and northeast Africa. Abbott recounts Alexander's major battles against the Persians and annexation of their empire. The book also examines Alexander's tactics, military innovations, and creation of a Hellenistic empire stretching from Greece to India before his death at 32.

Alfred the Great: This biography focuses on Alfred's defense of the Kingdom of Wessex against Viking raids in 9th century England. It discusses how Alfred drove back the Great Heathen Army and then negotiated terms with the Vikings, designating parts of England for their settlement. Abbott also highlights Alfred's efforts to revive learning and education in England, as well as his codification of laws and strengthening of the Anglo-Saxon navy. The book frames Alfred as a scholarly, strategic and devout ruler whose achievements laid the foundation for a unified England.

King Charles I: This book looks at the reign of Charles I leading up to and during the English Civil War. It focuses on the religious and political conflicts between Charles I and Parliament, caused largely by Charles' belief in divine right of kings and many unpopular, authoritarian policies. Abbott also examines Charles' refusal to compromise, leading to the war against Parliament's New Model Army and his eventual execution for treason in 1649 under Oliver Cromwell.

King Charles II: This biography deals with the restoration of the English monarchy under Charles II after the death of Oliver Cromwell. It follows Charles II's return from exile and re-establishment of royal power. However, Abbott also notes Charles' own conflicts with Parliament and religious controversies during his reign. The book discusses Charles' hedonistic lifestyle and many mistresses, but also his support for science, exploration and trade that helped expand the British Empire.

ABOUT JACOB ABBOTT

Cleopatra: This book examines Cleopatra VII's life and rule over ancient Egypt. Abbott chronicles Cleopatra's relationships and political alliances with Julius Caesar and Mark Antony, as she sought to maintain Egypt's independence from Rome. The biography highlights Cleopatra's intelligence, education and strategic skills in dealing with Rome. But it ultimately focuses on Cleopatra's downfall and suicide after Mark Antony's defeat by Octavian, leading to Egypt becoming a Roman province.

Cyrus the Great: This biography covers Cyrus II of Persia, founder of the Achaemenid Empire. Abbott traces Cyrus's rise from Persian prince, to revolt against the Medes, to conqueror of the Lydian and Babylonian empires. The book also examines Cyrus's leadership qualities and tolerant policies toward conquered peoples. It portrays Cyrus as a wise, inspirational leader who created the model of a centralized Persian state.

Darius: This book looks at the reign of Darius I, examining his consolidation of the Persian Empire through administrative reforms, development of infrastructure, and expansion of territory. Abbott discusses Darius's division of the empire into provinces and implementation of a uniform tax system and coinage. The biography also covers his invasion of Greece which was thwarted at the famous Battle of Marathon. Overall, it presents Darius as an capable, pragmatic ruler under whom the Persian Empire reached its zenith.

Queen Elizabeth: This biography celebrates the long and prosperous reign of Queen Elizabeth I of England. Abbott focuses on Elizabeth's shrewd leadership, religious compromise, and patronage of the arts and literature that fostered English Renaissance culture. The book also highlights Elizabeth's naval defeat of the Spanish Armada which secured England's independence from Europe. Overall, Abbott portrays Elizabeth as a commanding, canny and popular female ruler who strengthened England as a major world power.

ABOUT JACOB ABBOTT

Genghis Khan: This book looks at the incredible rise of Temüjin, better known as Genghis Khan. It follows his hardships as an outcast youth to becoming the fearsome founder of the Mongol Empire. Abbott chronicles Genghis Khan's brilliant military tactics and utterly ruthless conquests that allowed the Mongols to dominate much of Asia and Eastern Europe. Overall it paints him as a complex figure--strategic genius but also brutal tyrant.

Hannibal: This biography focuses on the great Carthaginian general Hannibal Barca. It recounts his famous crossing of the Alps with war elephants and invasion of Italy during the Second Punic War against Rome. Abbott details Hannibal's victories in major battles like Cannae but also his eventual defeat by Scipio and exile. The book celebrates Hannibal's daring military prowess but also concession late in life that Rome could not be conquered.

Josephine: This book examines the life of Josephine Bonaparte from her aristocratic upbringing in Martinique to her marriage to Napoleon Bonaparte. It focuses on Josephine's time as Empress consort of France and her support for arts and education. But it also discusses Napoleon's eventual divorce from her due to dynastic pressures. Overall the book presents Josephine as an intelligent, compassionate woman who tempered some of Napoleon's ambition.

Julius Caesar: This traces Caesar's life from early military campaigns to dictator and eventual assassination. Abbott covers Caesar's conquest of Gaul, rivalry with Pompey, famously crossing the Rubicon and crowning as dictator. The biography also examines the conspiracy led by Brutus and Cassius to assassinate Caesar in order to save the Roman Republic. In all, the book presents Caesar as an unmatched military mind who irrevocably changed the Roman Empire.

Margaret of Anjou: This biography looks at Margaret of Anjou who became queen consort to England's King Henry VI. It focuses on the political intrigue and machinations Margaret became involved in to support her husband's reign during the War of the Roses. Abbott portrays Margaret as a fiercely devoted, cunning woman who backed the Lancastrians against factions like the Yorkists led by Richard Neville. Though she lost power, the book frames her as a dominant figure during the conflict.

Mary, Queen of Scots: This book examines the life of Mary Stuart who became Queen of Scotland as an infant. It follows her tumultuous reign marked by scandals and plots to overthrow her by Protestants. Her Catholicism also put her at odds with England's Elizabeth I. Abbott recounts Mary's forced abdication, escape to England, and eventual execution ordered by Elizabeth for plotting against her. Overall it presents a tragic figure whose life was marked by political and religious turmoil.

Nero: This biography looks at the notorious Roman emperor Nero. It explores his self-indulgent lifestyle and tyrannical rule marked by possible matricide and the brutal execution of Christians. Abbott also examines legends around Nero like his fiddling during the Great Fire of Rome. The book presents a despotic, unstable man who drastically weakened the Roman Empire.

Peter the Great: This book covers the reforms and policies of Peter the Great that rapidly westernized Russia. Abbott discusses Peter's extensive European travels as a youth and later programs to remake Russia's army, expand its naval fleet, and build a new capital in St. Petersburg. The biography also examines Peter's harsh, authoritarian approach to governing that consolidated his power. Overall it presents him as a pivotal, transformative tsar.

Pyrrhus: This examines the life and military exploits of Pyrrhus, king of Epirus. It focuses on his campaigns against Rome where he won major battles but suffered heavy losses, giving rise to the term "Pyrrhic victory." Abbott recounts Pyrrhus's struggles to build a Greek empire and failed invasion of Sicily against Carthage. Though a skilled commander, Pyrrhus ultimately failed to achieve lasting gains.

Richard I: This biography looks at the reign of Richard I, known as Lionheart. It focuses on Richard's leadership during the Third Crusade to recapture Jerusalem from Saladin. Abbott also details the legendary tales of Richard's bravery and valor in campaigns against France and during his imprisonment. Overall, the book presents Richard I as one of England's great warrior kings.

Richard II: This explores the reign and overthrow of King Richard II. Abbott covers Richard's despotic actions that led the nobles to revolt and install Henry IV, leading to Richard's imprisonment and likely murder. The biography presents a weak king whose tyranny and poor leadership during a peasant's revolt cost him power and his life.

Richard III: This delves into the controversial rule of Richard III. Abbott examines Richard's contested path to the throne and the disappearance of the Princes in the Tower which Richard likely ordered. It also portrays Richard's defeat at the hands of Henry Tudor at the Battle of Bosworth Field that ended the Wars of the Roses. Ultimately Abbott paints Richard III as willing to employ any means to gain and retain the English crown.

Romulus: This recounts the Roman legend of Romulus and Remus, twin brothers raised by a she-wolf who went on to found the city of Rome. Abbott covers the myths of the brothers' quarrel over leadership, with Romulus killing Remus and becoming Rome's first king and architect of its nascent political institutions. Though mythological, Romulus represents ancient Rome's founding origins and rise to power.

William the Conqueror: This biography follows William, Duke of Normandy's conquest of England in 1066 after victory at the Battle of Hastings. Abbott discusses William's reign as king where he consolidated control, introduced feudalism, and fused English and Norman culture. William is presented as a formidable, innovative Norman leader who irrevocably transformed Anglo-Saxon England.

Xerxes: This examines the reign of Xerxes I of Persia, known for his failed invasion of Greece. Abbott focuses on Xerxes's gathering of a massive army to crush Greek resistance, but defeat at Salamis ended his ambitions. The book covers later unrest and palace intrigue that clouded the end of Xerxes's reign. Overall he is portrayed as a rash ruler whose desire for conquest led to disaster for Persia.

Abbott continued writing up until his death on October 31, 1879 in Farmington, Maine. His legacy lives on through his contributions to 19th century children's literature.

www.ingramcontent.com/pod-product-compliance
Lightning Source LLC
Chambersburg PA
CBHW070101080526
44586CB00013B/1147